The Republic of the Poor

Keepers of the rusted Coins

I0437783

Kahabi G. Isangula

P.o.Box 1252, Shinyanga,Tanzania.+255
Tel:+255754030726
E-Mail: kaisa079@yahoo.com

ISBN-10: **1500372161**
ISBN-13: **978-1500372163**

Acknowledgements

Firstly, I would like to thank my wife, Neema, for her love, encouragement, support and patience during the time it has got hold of me to write this book. Secondly, My son, Evan and my daughter, Eileen, for whom a desire for a more beneficial future for them motivated me to compose this book. Thirdly, the Acumen East African Fellowship program for a learning opportunity that shaped the direction of this book. Fourthly, Sarah Matindi (Kenya), Cory Rodgers (USA) and Callen Omurwa (USA) for editorial work without which readers' understanding of my wisdom would have been significantly restricted. Lastly, I would like to thank to you all for reading this book.

To my son, Evan and daughter, Eileen,
Your struggles in life will earn you gold coins!

To the poor, whose life motivates me to write!

Table of contents

The Poor.
Meaning and Context

The republic of the poor,
Houses with no doors,
In sorrows every hour,
For thee robbed powers.
Bodies with no pain,
Both hands in chains,
When others gain,
Keepers of the rusted coins!

  Imagine a republic - not the Plato's republic, but a true republic of mine, perhaps yours too or even your friend's in a very distant country. In this republic there are different people, or what we often call citizens: men and women, children and adults, the rich and the so-called poor. Today, let's continue to imagine that this republic is only the republic of the so-called poor, with men and women, children and adults of course.

  I realize that throughout your childhood and perhaps adulthood, the word 'poor' has been ringing bells in your ears endlessly. If you were lucky, it may have been your nanny who used this as a reference when motivating you to finish the food on your plate. Or perhaps, it was central to the narrative of your gifted parents, who informed you that, in comparison to your good fortune, they had nothing to eat when they were kids. You have heard this word in schools, churches,and mosques, read it in newspapers, articles, and reports, referenced it in politics,debates, constitutions and countless other sources. With the assumption that you don't know what you don't know, the fact that you know the existence of the poor - and you are perhaps imagining or considering yourself as one - simply means that the poor are everywhere. It is like the air we breathe. Do not worry my friend, for if you haven't heard this word before, then I have just told you.

One of the most common problems we have is defining the poor. Let me start by looking at some of the various attempts, not because I assume that you don't know but simply because the discussion in this book is grounded on these conceptualizations.

Globally, the economists, researchers, strategists, politicians and others refer to economic deprivation when referring to the poor. The United Nations, as per articles in 1995 and 2010, and a 2005 article by Gordon, defined the poor as those people who are unable access opportunities and make their own choices. Gordon considers poverty itself as a violation of human dignity. The poor, according the United Nations, lacks the basic capacity to participate effectively in the society. They do not have *enough* food and clothing, they do not have schools or clinics to go to, they do not have the land on which to grow their food or a job to earn a living, and they have no access to credit. This means that they are *insecure* and *powerless*. The poor are *susceptible* to violence and live in marginal or fragile environments, without access to clean water or sanitation.

Some of the key aspects of this definition conflicts with observations of the poor who live in this republic, particularly the *rural poor*. "Our poor" have lands to grow their crops, though they may not produce enough; they have clothes, though old ones; they have schools, though their children are uneducated; they have clinics, though they may be several kilometers away and perhaps the medicines may be scarce;

and some of them live only kilometers away from water sources though the water may not be clean and safe.

The World Bank on the other hand, (Coudouel and colleagues,2002), defines a poor person as one who is deprived of well-being, and this deprivation comprises many dimensions. The dimensions of deprivation encompass income and the ability to acquire the basic goods and services necessary for survival with dignity. A poor person also has low levels of health and education, poor access to clean water and sanitation, inadequate physical security, lack of voice (*powerlessness*), and insufficient capacity and opportunity to better his or her own life.

The Copenhagen Declaration (Woodward,2010), introduced the term '*absolute poverty*' which classified a poor person as one severely lacking basic needs, such as food, safe drinking water, sanitation facilities, health, shelter, education and information. The declaration identified poverty as not only income related but also a lack of access to social services.

In Siegel and Yacht's Personal Finance Book (2009), poverty is defined in opposition to wealth according to a measure of accumulated profit, or the difference between one's income and expenses. That is, by this definition, if you have borrowed some money to invest in something, your debt can be considered a liability that makes you less wealthy, even if you have diversified and secure investments. And if the difference between your income and expenses-plus-debt is small, you might as well be considered poor. This definition also excludes most of the wealthier people we know in our republic, those with hundreds of cows or other liquid assets that can be utilized whenever there is an expense to be incurred such as a sickness in the family. Many forms of traditional African investments do not fit with Siegel and Yacht's simple definition, revealing their Western bias.

I am not entirely opposed to these definitions or measures of poverty on all counts, but it is my intent to change your thinking if you are a believer in these.

Few of us have thought of this from an entirely different angle, taking stock of our own experiences with poverty - whether those be acquired by living in it or by observing those who, to date, still live in it. I would define the poor - particularly in our republic - not by *economic* measures but by *capability* measures. Today, I will walk you through the basics of this alternative definition, challenging those who insist upon the doctrine of poverty-as-low-income. I must warn you, however, that if you are a believer in *quantifications,* your heart may be broken, for while an income-based measure allows you to quantify the income index - say a dollar a day - capability measures require an index of "thinking capacity" that you cannot quantify with such simple ratio; for example, a thought a day.

The non-quantitative nature of a capability index is no reason to disregard its critical application in conceptualizing the poor in our republic. Observations and contextual descriptions acquired and processed with careful reasoning or thought, allow us to confidently provide explanations and generate arguments about the situations in which we find ourselves in our society. As Jean Jacques Rousseau (1972) explains through his notion of *social contract,* the fact that things are as they are does not mean that it is how they are supposed to be. Just because the poor are defined by the income measures globally, it does not mean that is how they are supposed to be defined. People are naturally believers of the stories that dominate their lives as they grow and interact with one another, and they will tell the same stories as if they were the originators when they continue to interact with new people. I agree with Thomas Hobbes's *The Leviathan (*1651) that human nature condemns to us but only human reason can save us.

To define the poor, let me begin by examining the ways that we not only observe and define them, but look down upon them.. There is a story a famous leader of a certain country who was visiting one of the rural areas. When crossing one of the forests, he saw a large number of villagers who were defecating in the forest, both adults and children. He felt sorry for these people, particularly an old lady who was left naked when, upon noticing that the car was approaching her direction, she fled into the forest and got her cloth trapped on tree bark. The image of this woman kept revolving in the head of this leader even when he went back to his mansion in the city. The next day he ordered his servants to go and build nice toilets in that village. Yes, after a month or so, photos of modern toilets in a rural village decorated the newspapers and televisions, and the leader was proclaimed a hero and savior of the poor. Media testimonials were overwhelming, with video clips of women proclaiming to be saved from poisonous snake bites and children celebrating in relief at the convenience.Husbands proclaimed their wives would now be faithful because women having affairs with other men in the forest could no longer use defecation as a decoy. The stories survived to the re-election of the leader, and thereafter the village was forgotten as if it never existed.

After three years or so, when the leader went back to the same village, he found that the number of villagers who use the forest for their "after-meal service" had almost tripled and to his surprise, the so-called toilets were now being used for cereal storage. The villagers had even established a register to record everyone's sacks of cereals. When the leader asked why they turned modern toilets that had costed him so much money into stores, the villagers responded that they failed to use the toilets for mainly three reasons: first, since childhood, they had been going into the forest and they have not noticed any harm coming to them. Secondly, the lack of toilets was not as great a problem as finding a place where they could keep their cereals safe from rotting particularly in the rainy season and out of the reach of giant rats. Thirdly, water scarcity in the village made it difficult to maintain maximum hygiene at the toilets. Children had started having diarrhea after using the toilets, the foul smell and mega flies emanating from the toilets had become a disturbance to the villagers during their lunchtime meals, which were always served outside the houses under a big tree.

There were other reasons too; the villagers were not trained to wash up properly, which is a prerequisite for the modern toilet unlike the simple, slimy leaves that would otherwise be used in the forest. For those who did wash up, they suffered from fungal infections as a result of using the water from a village dam. Also, the distance of the toilets from some of the households posed the challenge, some took two kilometers to reach the toilets - you can imagine what would happen if someone experienced aggravated abdominal motions. Despite these critical reasons, the poor villagers were looked upon as people who do not understand what was important to them, people who had needs that they did not comprehend or know how to address.

We, the experts, are beholden to a culture of labeling and tagging those who fail to do what we expected them to do as per our scholastic judgements. This observation is supported by Grundy & Anner (2010) when reporting on health care seeking behaviors (HSB) in one of the low income country. They asserts that, "Many [experts] seem to adopt theoretical assumptions based on a cause-and-effect understanding of the relationship between specific knowledge, attitudes and practices and health behaviors and outcomes. In this sense, the [poor] or community then becomes a 'target' of 'interventions' from expert practitioners and organizations equipped with an assumed superior set of knowledge, attitudes and behaviors. This language, which is common to public health reflects the dominance of expert opinion in the proposed modelling of healthy behaviors" (p.10)

Similarly, even those who are considered rich have the stories of their poverty. I am reminded of the time when I listened to the renowned and beautiful Nigerian author Chimamanda Ngozi Adichie speaking at TED in 2009 on the 'The danger of a single story'. Although I won't dwell long on her story that has inspired many of us to write our own stories, I will just use a portion of her talk to illustrate my point. Illustrative of her definition of the poor is her story of butter disappearing from bread and other things of the sort, unlike most of us who came across a bread in our teen age.

Indeed, poverty is a very subjective word - it may refer to absolute deprivation of basic needs or what Plato calls the necessities of life: food, life, dwelling and clothing (all of which are always linked to income measures). The deprivation may also be in terms of what Article Three of *The Universal Declaration of Human Rights* call 'life, liberty and security'. However, being poor is indicative of conditions beyond inadequate necessities.In contrast, those of us who define poverty in terms of capability measures believe that the label "poor" refers to those people with deprivation of basic individual capabilities, not merely low income. It is a deprivation of capabilities to fulfill personal development. Personal development here means freedom of persons to fulfilling their potential in such areas as life, work, and education, and so on in the context of the value they assign to these potentials and which they experience in their actions. Aung San Suu Kyi offered this logical definition in 1945.

Different people such as politicians, economists, researchers and even the poor themselves, see the poor differently. A politician would often concur with economists and the World Bank in their income-dictated definition of poverty, which is, living below a dollar and 25cents a day. The very same people would talk about *purchasing power*: the financial ability of people to buy products and services. Others would talk of *economic productivity*: the ratio of output to inputs in production that measures the production efficiency. "The Poor" becomes people whose low productivity at the individual level negatively affects statistics of national productivity.

However, those of us who believe in capability measures believe that low productivity at the individual level is directly linked to deprivation in individual capabilities. You will agree with me that poverty is not just deprivation of capabilities but also *chronic* deprivation of capabilities. This *chronicity* is a consequence of deprivation in the mental aspects of the human being - that is, the brain - which results from complex interrelated factors and would lead to what is called *'poverty of the mind or thought'* - the inability to thinking and reason well. This poverty of the mind/thought entraps people in the vicious cycle of poverty, and as a result, a person believes that there is nothing he or she can do to emerge from that cycle. My argument is that **income poverty is secondary to poverty of the thought.** Poverty of the thought or mind is a precursor of economic poverty.

For those of you who have experience or at least knowledge of the rural lifestyle, I would bet that you have passed by natural forests in rural villages. I believe too that you have seen poor houses around or near these forests. You may have wondered why people could be so poor despite their proximity to these rich natural forests. These are the same forests from which materials such as timber are harvested and used to make furniture in five star hotels in the city. Of course, in cities we do not keep forests and thus, the timbers come from non-urban areas. These kinds of people, who leave near natural resources, are considered as economically poor because of their poverty of the thought - *their inability to explore the resources around them and make use of them to improve their lives.* They are entrapped in this situation and become people who wait for saints such as governments, non-governmental entities or experts to 'save' them and perhaps build houses for them. They may become shocked if they one day come to the city and happen to see beautiful furniture in hotels. It is like a fisherman who would be amazed by the buffet in a hotel in which his fish is one of the items served or a banana farmer surprised to learn that bananas from his farm are the ingredients in an elaborate plantain dish at an urban restaurant, as well as a mango tree farmer amazed by a cold mango juice in the city that was made from the fruit of his own farm.

The poverty of the thought also affects how the poor *choose* to deal or *respond* to their needs. Although I will cover this in the next lesson, as human beings, we have two kinds of needs: first, there are *immediate needs* that, if met, will relieve an individual from troubles, pain or suffering, either physical or emotional, for few hours, days or weeks. The other type of needs are what I call *sustainability needs;* the type of needs that, when addressed, will consequently address the immediate needs in the long run and other needs that may arise in the future.

The immediate needs are similar to what Maslow (1943) refers to in his *Motivational Theories as* 'physiological needs', which are the lowest level needs in influential hierarchy. These needs include *survival* requirements such as food, water, clothing and so on. *People with poverty of thought spend most of their time focusing on addressing these needs, and they are likely to accept any opportunity to address them.* A person who only focuses on these needs is driven to make choices for the sake of *survival* that other people may deem wrong. As Leslie Radford(2001) clearly explains in *Motivation* article, a hungry person has a felt need that sets up both psychological and physical tensions that manifest in overt behaviors directed at reducing those tensions. These tensions may result in actions normally considered immoral or illogical by many. For example, stealing items from other people or selling his political votes for a kilo of rice during electoral campaigns. Unlike Maslow who comments that once the physiological needs are addressed the tension is reduced, and the need ceases to motivate, I hold a view that as long as the poverty of the thought exists, a person will continue to make the same choices just to survive. *Survival becomes the ultimate purpose in his life.* He would always worship over material support provided by the 'saviors' of the poor.

On the other hand, those people who aspire to get

themselves out of poverty entrapment or even those who wish not to enter the entrapment often focus upon sustainability needs. These needs have different key drivers that are often derived from different experiences. These drivers motivate those people who we often believe are born with a 'natural' desire to focus on success. Often cited examples are the Chagga tribe in Tanzania and perhaps the Kikuyu in Kenya who are sometimes thought to possess *natural entrepreneurial* behaviors. This prejudice operates in their favor. As the child grows in these tribes, his life experiences are programmed in such a way that the word 'success' is painted on his or her face. They are capable of foreseeing opportunities for success in the future. For example, they may invest during their lives, in relationships with people who are economically poor but more likely to be financially successful in the future. This only depicts that these people have certain 'strengths' in their thought process and a form of programmed thinking that exceeds via foresight, that of a person who seeks to address immediate needs. Their primary focus is to address sustainability needs often at the expense of immediate needs.

Human beings are equal but differ in strengths both physical and mental in form of programmed thoughts. Thomas Hobbes in *The Leviathan*, comments that although men are naturally equal, they have different physical strengths; such is the case with the 'strength' of their thoughts. This simply means, although we are born free and equal - as The Universal Declaration of Human Rights affirms - people can still differ in terms of strengths. These 'mental' strengths as well as physical strengths are often *limited by circumstances* in people whose primary focus is immediate needs. They would, for example, trade their votes for material handouts during election. As evidence, consider how politicians often distribute material handouts such as t-shirts to people whose immediate need is cloth, kilos of rice to people whose immediate need is food, or local beers to people whose immediate need is getting drunk. All these people, due to their poverty of thought would always trade their vote to the person who offers alleviation of their immediate needs.

Poverty of the thought is not only limited to economically poor people, but also some of the educated or even the economically able individuals. Though academic intelligence works for many, it may not necessarily mean good divergent and convergent thinking. However, as I said earlier, there are multiple factors that interact to affect poverty of thought. The most common factor is education. While education is the basic drive to eliminate poverty of thought, the nature or content of education on the other hand can in contradiction , drive people into it.

I am of the view that most education systems in poor republics have mixed outcomes, driving few out of the poverty of thought and at the same time driving many into it. It does this by programming them to respond to short-term challenges such as examinations instead of responding to long-term life problems. A graduate's primary purpose would be to get employed as much as to address his or her immediate needs for food, shelter and most often transport. After being employed s/he would often take company loan to buy a car or a plot, often in a very distant outskirt of the town. If s/he rushes to build a small house and start a life with family and kids, then the family-related demands would actually place him/her into the entrapment of *the educated poor* which is not, by the most pertinent measures, different from the entrapment of the poor. The educated poor are similarly likely to start taking actions that are considered immoral - such as taking bribes - or illogical - such as supporting a political party that creates only short-term opportunities to address his/her immediate needs. This is because the resources at their disposal can neither sustain their family nor extended dependants.

The difference between the educated poor and the poor is of course, the fact that the poor have resources but they cannot innovatively use these resources to address their needs while on the other hand, the educated poor has strived to use their resources for education, but entrapped themselves into this kind of poverty by only seeking to address immediate needs.

Perhaps you have not understood what I am trying to say here. An example would be when I was in elementary school, our art teacher would score lower those students who submitted handmade items for an assignment while scoring higher those who submitted readymade items such as cups or jars. I guess he was trying to address his immediate need for utensils at his home. By his actions, he did not only blunt innovation but also reinforced and programmed non-creativity among children from a very young age. I remember being among the students whose scores were very low in art class, which resulted in my tendency to distance myself from anything with signs of 'art' during my time in school. I could have been a professional craftsman by now - something I still desire - but the education process and the teacher, who was supposed to promote my desires to propagate my talent, did not nurture me.

The educated poor can be expected to develop into 'poor' experts, 'poor' workers, and most unfortunate, 'poor' politicians, should they find their way into politics. Leaders in many republics are the products of such education systems, which promote a focus on immediate needs. As a result, processes that facilitate an individual to focus on addressing sustainability needs and creativity are limited in our schools. Students dwell upon these needs and, much worse, graduates dream of a job that would help them address these needs and acquire food, shelter and other immediate necessities.

These people, the educated poor, may opt to pursue a career in politics because it is often seen a way to address these needs quickly. The liberation of our republic from the chains of poverty may therefore not be the primary motivation behind their political activities, but these politicians may hide their true intentions by manipulating the rest of the poor with handouts and promises, all for the sake of getting elected and re-elected. The poor, imprisoned by the poverty of thought, cannot -,as Chinua Achebe puts it , *compel their leaders to greatness or even demand basic competences from them.*

People with poverty of the mind always focus on survival; they choose any option that seems to bring hope for survival. The people with poverty of thought are thereby rendered powerless and without voice. *Powerlessness* is at least one thing I can borrow from the economic definitions of poverty. Power, used in this context as Aung Suu defined it, entails an ability to express and impose one's will in a given social relation and in the face of an unfavorable situation. The people with the poverty of the thought are incapable of either imposing or coercing their leaders in their 'social' relationship, which in this case constitutes the leadership role itself. They form a *republic* - a republic of powerless and very fearful individuals - and often politicians use this to their advantage.

The educated poor who find their way into political positions reinforce this fear by preaching the importance of peace, a way of protecting their own interests since they will be on the losing end if the status quo is changed. They face the threat of becoming the first target, should the poor start demanding power and accountability. The educated poor may convince their poor constituents not to elect leaders from an opposing group by explaining that they will bring problems. In the worst of circumstances, the educated poor may also use the forces at their disposal to plot terrifying events that would reinforce fear and powerlessness among the poor, reinforcing the idea that opposing groups will bring terror to the republic.

Julius Nyerere's ideology on development for example,entails that to develop; a country needs people, land, leadership and good politics. On the other hand, a country with people and land but weak leadership and dirty politics will never develop. Likewise, if people have land but they do not have the power or drive to use land as a resource to address their sustainability needs − rather than immediate needs - they will always remain poor in their republic.

In order to alleviate poverty of the mind, Aung San Suu suggests, *setting in motion the process which can change perception* as a product of thought. This entails changing thought of people in this situation, the poor. Material supports cannot liberate the poor from their cycle of poverty entrapment. Liberation must begin by freeing people from the poverty inherent in thoughts of powerlessness, helplessness, inefficiency and inadequacy. People need to be empowered to explore and use the available resources innovatively to address their sustainability needs, while at the same time holding their leaders accountable and demanding tangible deliverables from them. If there is no one capable of empowering the poor, then they need to find ways to empower themselves - individually or in groups. Empowering oneself begins by looking at the resources available and using them creatively to liberate oneself from the chains of poverty. In groups, the powerless become powerful...just look at the ways that small weekly offerings are building beautiful churches in the republic.

It is my belief that you have comprehended my arguments about poverty of thought. I expect many readers to deny these arguments - as that is one of the basic characteristics of the educated poor, of which you, my reader, are none of them perhaps.

Further Reading

1. Aung San Suu Kyi.A Culture of Peace, Democracy, and Human Rights. 1945.
2. Chimamanda Ngozi Adichie. The danger of a single story. TEDGlobal 2009.
3. Chinua Achebe. The University and the Leadership Factor in Nigerian Politics. Abic Books & Equipment.1988.
4. Coudouel et al.Poverty Measurement and Analysis, in the PRSP Sourcebook, World Bank, Washington D.C. 2002.
5. Gordon, D.Indicators of Poverty and Hunger, Presentation to Expert Group Meeting on Youth Development Indicators, United Nations Headquarters, New York. 2005.
6. Grundy J, Annear P. Health-Seeking Behaviour Studies: a Literature Review of Study Design and Methods with a Focus on Cambodia Australia: University of Melbourne, The Nossal Institute for Global Health; 2010
7. Jean Jacques Rousseau: The Social Contract or Principles of Political Right. 1972.
8. Julius Nyerere: Freedom and Development. Oxford University Press.1973.
9. Leslie Radford. *Motivation.* Available at http://www.mindtools.com/pages/article/newLDR_84.htm, Understanding leadership styles
10. Maslow, A. H. A theory of human motivation. Psychological Review, 1943: 50(4), 370–96.
11. Rachel Siegel & Carol Yacht: Personal Finance. Flat world Knowledge.2009.
12. Plato. The Republic. Cambridge University Press.2000
13. Thomas Hobbes. The Leviathan. Chapter XIII: Of the Natural Condition of Mankind as concerning their felicity and misery. 1651.
14. United Nations: Universal Declaration of Human Rights. 1948, December 10th.
15. United Nations. The Copenhagen Declaration and Programme of Action, World Summit for Social Development, 6-12 March 1995, New York, United Nations.
16. United Nations. The Millennium Development Goals Report, New York, United Nations.2010.
17. Woodward, D. How Poor is 'Poor'? Towards a Rights-based Poverty Line, London, New Economics Foundation. 2010.

LESSON TWO

The Poor.
Thoughts and Powerlessness

Lost smiles, lost hopes
Lost thoughts, the thoughtless minds
Lost fate, lost future
Lost citizens, the powerless wits
Lost votes, lost leaders
A lost right, a lost republic!

By now, I would assume you agree with me that poverty of the mind is a precursor to economic poverty. A number of economists have challenged my stand long before I was born and many will do even when I am still alive. The economists have come up with hundreds of economic *models* to alleviate poverty, but if you ask whether these models have worked in any republic of the poor, you would receive the demoralizing answers that nothing has really been practical.

A common measure of economic growth is the annual percent change in gross domestic product. Leaders of the republic of the poor look to this measure and believe that there is economic growth. However, for quite some time, the so-called growth has been increasing by mere decimal amounts. Much worse, the lives of the poor remain stagnant, and they cannot sense the so-called change in economic growth. Likewise, there have been so many efforts to 'save' the poor such as debt reliefs and external budget support programs to the republics of the poor, not to mention the influx of international Non-Governmental Organizations and experts who deal with the so-called systems strengthening. The experts are sent to train the poor on reproductive rights, disease control and even how to take care of their excrements after eating donated meals. These efforts have been insignificantly fruitful. The poor are increasingly impoverished while the so-called the rich are competing for the Forbes list. The poor will always use the old, rusted coins, even when the National Bank changes the currency of the republic.

The situation, you see, simply means that we are all different! Some of the economic principles that seem to work well in Western countries cannot be applied in developing countries. For this reason, many West-driven economic solutions have proved only mildly fruitful in developing republics. I would argue that we are at different stages of what I shall call *thought growth* levels. One of the main pieces of evidence of the different stages of thought growth is the desire to pay tax. I have lived in the West, and I have seen that while, on the one hand, people in the west feel the pride of paying taxes, on the other hand, most Africans feel pride in *escaping tax*. The different stages of thought process have enabled the west to create strong democratic mechanisms that they can use to hold their governments accountable for their taxes, while in the republics of the poor, people who benefit from the small tax that is being collected blindly oppose efforts to create mechanisms for accountability. Likewise, the poor do not see their taxes translating into personal-level development.

The simplistic meaning behind this observation is that people are 'powerless' in the sense that they cannot influence tax policy, yet they are also fearful in the sense that they do not believe they can hold their governments accountable for budgetary spending. As stated in the previous section, people with poverty of the mind are powerless, fearful and unable to sufficiently demand even the most basic of competencies from their leaders. In order to feel pride in paying taxes to the government, they must believe that they have the power to hold it accountable for the tax expenditures.

The power that individuals perceive in them not only fosters competence and accountability among leaders or even civil servants; it also drives demand for quality in the services offered to the public. In one of my books, *A Leaking Needle,* I proposed that the quality of health services is mostly improved if the citizens who seek that service *demand* a high level of quality. In areas where there are poor services or infrastructures, if tax payers fail to demand quality services and improved infrastructures, no one will ever improve such situation unless there are other personal motives or aspirations that self-coerce an individual leader to make improvements. Leader's motives to make improvement are many but just to give an example, is when there is a visit by a most powerful figure in the area or when the general election is approaching. We have seen buildings being painted, hospitals being improved, roads being constructed just because someone powerful from central government is coming and not because the people deserves quality services and infrastructure.

Another example is when the President of United States of America visited Africa towards in 2013 and 2015. Most republics instituted emergency plans to improve the environment and infrastructures particularly in areas where the president would pass or visit. All the roads were renovated or mopped and the streets were dusted, painted and cleared on account of his arrival. Beggars who would always disturb the common citizens were cleared off the streets. The same was observed when the former president Bush visited several countries in Africa. This was done not because roads and street needs to be clean, but because a very important person was coming. After these important people have gone back to their countries, things turns back to the way they were and much worse, 'the welcome to the republic' posters are left to fall off themselves from posts and walls across the stress making things much worse than before. People never complained and never demanded for making this a routine instead of waiting for visitors.

This behavior begins at the family level. For example when I was very young- I remember the first time to put a shirt on my bare chest was a time when there Uhuru Torch ceremonies were to be held in my village. That was the first time my father, who was one of the member in a village council bought a shirt that was unfortunately large to my size, but I enjoyed it anyway. It's the same day during which I applied a body lotion after taking a bath. The next time I had another shirt was three years later when the top leader of the republic would visit my village to inaugurate a village water pump. Unfortunately, like many others, I never complained. It had never occurred to me that wearing a shirt was my basic right and that walking bare chest was not what I deserved and instead, I accepted the shirt as if it was a favor from my father. I could have demanded a new shirt perhaps every month. This is how we are programmed to seeing our basic rights as favors.

As I said, this operant conditioning roots from family levels. We keep our houses neat when expecting some important visitors not because our houses need to be clean all the time. A man living single would keep himself smart when expecting a date not because he is supposed to look smart every day. People are conditioned from young age to respond on these expectancy circumstances by improving their situation - not because *they see a need* to improve their situations to meet their own needs. Leaders become accustomed to improve services and infrastructures in response to visitors from higher levels or outside the country not because citizens need such improvements- since the citizens are so powerless to demand quality.

The demand for quality, competence and accountability in countries where people are powerless is often tasked to the third party monitoring entities that I would describe in the coming sections. These entities often trouble themselves in creating a demand for quality, competence and accountability on behalf of citizens. In authoritative republics, these mechanisms are always blunt-ended as they are often squeezed to powerlessness. Often, most of them exists as economic ladder for their founders and are donor-dependent. For these mechanisms to be strong- absolute freedom is necessary and to a greater extent they need to be rooted from the people themselves. These entities need to focus on advocacy with the people, not advocacy for the people.

Culture has always promoted and continues to promote powerlessness. As the Universal Declaration of Human Rights states, 'every human being is born free and equal'- there is no one born as a businessman or a politician- these 'specializations' comes as we all struggle for personal excellence. In childhood, children may be discouraged from questioning certain things; for example if a seven year child asks his father why he has to share a bed with his mother, the consequences may be unbearable. A child who question guests for example, is considered; in many African cultures as disrespectful, as a result he may stop questioning at all! This programming is also depicted in schools where a student is not expected to differ with his teacher or instructor. The same culture is also encouraged in work places where the circumstances do not allow junior staff to question or challenge their bosses' decisions even if they are wrong.

When I was in secondary school for example, I was a victim of such 'culture'. I happened to have been exposed to course materials from one of a famous tuition teacher during annual break and when classes resumed, I was way ahead of the class in terms of the syllabus. When the Physics teacher made a mistake in one of the calculations, I challenged him in a very respectful way. Unexpectedly, I was expelled from Physics class for the whole year for challenging the teacher. The library became my teacher and I ended being the only one who scored an A in the National Exams for the subject.

The same teacher was rewarded for one of 'his students' (me) performing well for the first time.

Another key driver of powerlessness is self-image. A book called *Opening the door to your future* by Dan S. Kennedy (1995) defines it as *the image or picture you hold in your mind about yourself.* The book further comments that self-image is built by things your parents and siblings repeatedly said about you as you were growing up, things your friends and co-workers now say about you and comparisons you make between yourself and others.

Parents are key programmer of their children's self-image to become powerless later in their lives. Strict and protective parents and who teach a child to 'speak only when spoken to' or 'don't talk to strangers', creates a self-image of a person who cannot only challenge his seniors but also question their decisions even if those decisions affects him negatively, directly and indirectly , in the short or long term. These people from their young age would begin to choose activities that reinforce powerlessness such as sitting behind classroom, staying quiet or neutral at times when they are required to choose a side.

This programming does not only promote powerlessness but also inhibit creativity and critical thinking. If a child tries to ride his father's bicycle in the village and suffers an accident that would be the last day he would ride it due to the punishment that will be administered. He is then programmed to become fearful of the consequences as a result, he stop trying to ride a bicycle again. Likewise, this programming goes on into what is happening in schools where children are shamed for poor performances or failures. They then grow into adults who are afraid of taking risks as a result they became fearful, powerless and mere or average thinkers. As common or average thinkers who are fearful of the consequences of failures, they would mostly choose those activities that offer no failure options- often simple and immoral activities. At work, they would mostly choose to keep silent if the boss does something immoral for the fear of losing their jobs for example.

Another example is during civil workers strike. Often the government responds adversely- the government would say if you don't return to work you will lose your job and salary. People who have been programmed to be fearful and whose main focus is immediate needs, will return to work the next day because to them, loosing a job is too risky. Going back to work simply means they have surrendered the *rights* they were fighting for and choose to keep quiet indefinitely. They are accepting the status quo and are less likely to demand for more benefits or work improvements in the future.

Powerlessness makes people the 'minorities' not in the context of their numbers but in the context of their inability to hold authorities accountable. As documented by *Aung San Suu*, minorities are not only defined by numbers but also by underprivilegeness. Powerlessness shifts the status quo ;making the majority to become the minority and vice versa. The majority becomes minorities as they are estranged from power elite and are considered inferior. Likewise, the minority becomes the majority in this context, as they are powerful and make decisions for majority despite the fact that they are few, just because they consider themselves superior. The superiors may program the inferior many in such a way that they continue to maintain their status quo. The superiors would always do the unthinkable to maintain their needs. The needs that Maslow call *social needs* such as the desire for reputation, prestige, status, fame, glory, dominance, recognition, attention, importance, and appreciation.

Another source of powerlessness is the intelligence capacity. The poor, the powerless, have limited *fluid* and *crystallized intelligence*. Fluid intelligence, as defined by Charles Stangor in *Introduction to psychology* is the capacity to learn new ways of solving problems people face in daily life. The crystallized intelligence refers to the knowledge of the world people accumulates throughout their lives. A person with intact fluid and crystallized intelligence has higher analytical, creative and practical intelligences. Both the ability to learn new ways of solving problems and knowledge of the world is highly affected by the prevailing environmental, social, cultural and political factors.

Crystalized intelligence increases with age and this is what we often call wisdom. A person with limited exposure to the external world, a world outside his domicile, would always have limited learning opportunities as a result will accumulate conservative knowledge by only observing what is around him. That allows him to have limited thinking consequently weak analytical, creative and practical intelligence capacity. Practical intelligence or common sense entails the type of intelligence gained from informal learning, not from books or formal schools.

Scientists have argued that you do not necessarily need higher analytical intelligence to be creative. A person may be analytical but not creative and vice versa. Charles Stangor identifies five prerequisites for creativity. These are *expertise,* a deep understanding of what someone is working on; *imaginative thinking,* the ability to visualize the problem in a way that allows them to hold different points of view as well as different options or ideas for solutions; *risk taking,* the ability to experiment the solutions despite the uncertainties of risks of failure; *intrinsic interest,* the deep emotional drive for working towards the solution not because of the financial incentives and, *working in creative environment,* the environment that continually support creativity and challenge the creator.

These five factors, necessary for creativity, are almost always absent in communities perceived as poor. Expertise for example, is limited because the poor have scanty mechanisms for both informal and formal learning processes that are required to achieve expertise needed for creativity. The imaginative thinking aspect is limited by weak divergent and convergent intelligence. In these circumstances, risk avoidance is culturally and politically programmed and promoted as a profitable endevoir. The poor are culturally programmed in such a way that holding on to 'old ways' of doing things is considered as the appropriate option for achieving success. Of course, those who are risk takers are often considered as 'crazy'. Vibeke Venema of BBC World Service reported that when Arunachalam Muruganantham, a school dropout from a poor family in southern India invented sanitary pads that would late come to revolutionize menstrual health for rural women, he was considered crazy by fellow villagers. Much worse, his wife left when he was testing the invention. No woman would volunteer to wear them during testing phase thus; he decided to wear them himself despite developing them for women. This is common in areas where 'the poor' are dominant and is a setback to creativity.

Again, even the western countries have somehow, I may say, programmed the third world countries to become fearful of inventions or creativity. The republics in Africa for example, have a wealth of what I call *micro-inventions* that assists in solving daily life puzzles in conventional way. However, these items are only considered by the west as 'traditional' home decorations and not inventions. This makes the Africans powerless that they can only make traditional handcrafts regardless of the fact that these creative items were actually created to solve community problems. As such, people have been inclined to making 'traditional' items that suit the 'decoration needs' for the West instead of creating items that would solve local problems. One of my friends used to joke that the sorcery and witchcraft propagandas of the West have resulted to researchers not exploring the African-made items used for night-flying that could have perhaps solved the growing traffic jams. I know it was a joke, but a sensible one. The truth however remains that culture and external pressures have contributed to weakening the creative thinking particularly among the poor.

There are mixed views about being gifted or extremely smart. Some argue that being intelligent is a problem by itself. Others argue that smart people have adjustment problems and more difficult to create social relationships. I am gifted and among the comments I received after working for three organizations in five years, was that I was too pro-career development than what the organization can offer and as such, it was difficult to maintain healthy relationship with my bosses. In contrast, I held my own hypothesis on this: that, the environment in these organizations were not rewarding my efforts and often, whenever I excelled in terms of performance, the bosses became afraid that it may look like they are not contributing to the organization.

Terman and Oden in 1959 conducted a study on top one percent of students who scored 135 or higher in IQ tests. They noted that these students were healthier and well-adjusted compared to average students. Most of them achieved higher levels of education and entered prestigious professions. A follow up study by Seagoe in 1975 noted that they had good social relations and were less likely to be divorced than average person.

Some of the republics had at one time, what we used to call 'special schools' where such students, perceived as *gifted and talented* were provided with accelerated learning. Although most of these gifted graduates hold leadership positions in the republic, the socio-political environment has somehow contributed to not delivering excellence as it was expected of them. This has turned the academic enthusiasm and critical thinking seen in these schools into wasteful resources- the poor intellectuals. Although,some have excelled in whatever they are doing.

As I said earlier, the environment has a very significant impact on intelligence and creativity. It is believed that people who are smart have much bigger brains compared to others. McDaniel in 2005 reported that the neuroimaging studies by measuring brain sizes found a correlation between large brain size and intelligence which in turn correlated with the number of neurons and brain cortex thickness. Despite this fact, it may be illogical to believe that having a larger brain warrants high intelligence as all intelligence people in the world would have shown physical characteristics such as bigger head to accommodate bigger brains for example. However, it is believed that growing up in 'a stimulating 'environment that rewards thinking and learning may lead to a greater brain growth in terms of increased neurotisations (Garlick ,2003). Other factors such as good nutrition lead to increased brain growth and intelligence. Although the environment in which the poor lives may or may not be stimulating the thinking and learning processes in their brains, other factors such as poor nutrition in these settings fuels the negative consequences of environment on intelligence and creativity.

Intelligence is divided into two spheres: divergent and convergent.. Torasova, Volf & Razoumnikova in their 2010 article believe that the areas in the brain that deals with *convergence thinking*, thinking towards finding correct solutions to the problems are different from those dealing with the ability to generate many different solutions, ideas or options to a single problem, which is *divergent thinking*. However, the 'poor' often have limitations in both convergent and divergent thinking. When faced with a problem that requires a solution; their ability to generate different ideas and organize them into correct solutions is limited. As such, they would let *other* people who may not necessarily be from their community to generate ideas and select solutions for *their* problems. They become more powerless simply because they did not participate in developing the solution to their problem.

Intelligence is measured by what we call '*Intelligence Quotient*' in short 'IQ'. Environmental factors explain the variations in IQ for children from lower and higher socio economic classes. Although, I may hold a different view, it is evident that the upper class tends to provide an environment that is safe, supportive and a more nutritious meal. Since social and economic deprivation affects IQ significantly, Brooks –Gunn and Duncan in 1997 reported that children from poor families have lower IQs compared to those from resourceful families when other factors such as race, education and parenting are controlled. The diet of the poor may lack nutrients such as vitamins and protein as well as children being more likely to be exposed to environmental toxins or contaminants in drinking water or dusts (Bellinger and Needle-man 2013) and that all these environmental factors may slow brain development consequently reducing intelligence and critical thinking capabilities. Environment in the republic of the poor is also blamed for teratogens,with contributing factors such as air pollution and cigarettes particularly local cigar and alcohol containing substances that in large amount and prolonged exposure particularly at the more sensitive phases of growth in infancy may interfere with normal development. Mud houses with poor ventilation in which cooking is done indoors and shared with animals or birds is very common in areas where majority of people in the republic resides. In the same conditions few people would grow to become academically and economically successful but these comprises a very small percentage and are no motivations for people who continue living in these situations. This simply means that enriching environment is the ultimate solution to increase intelligence and creative thinking.

Scientists believes that intelligence is generally improved by education. According to Ceci in 1991, the number of years that a person spends in progressive school correlates with almost 60 percent of IQ. This may be due to the fact that people with higher IQ enjoys learning new things in order to gain expertise in the areas they are interested in more than people with lower IQs. You may argue that most of IQ tests are inclined towards formal education than informal education, however, the evidence on impact of informal learning on IQ is weak.

There are some aspects of intelligence that are highly influenced by informal or traditional learning. Informal learning is very important in *emotional intelligence*, the ability to accurately identify, assess and understand emotions as well as to effectively control emotions, as defined in R. J. Sternberg handbook. Generally, women have much higher emotional intelligence compared to men. In rural areas for example, as a result of informal emotional programming, women may control their expression of emotions of love to avoid being seen as prostitutes within the community. Conclusively, higher emotional intelligence does not equate to higher intelligence and creative thinking.

Emotions are closely related to *motivation*s. Motivations are the factors that act as driving forces that initiates or directs behavior. Maslow's theories of motivations have explained this in detail. Emotions play a key role in social behaviors. For example if we achieve something after a certain range of efforts we may feel emotions of joy and satisfaction and we are motivated to more likely repeat the same actions possibly intensifying the efforts. On the contrary, if we invest much effort into something but achieve less than our expectations, it is a human nature to choose behaviors that demotivates us from engaging in the same activity. This is a common trend in the republic, thus, failure warrants *not repeating the same activity* and thus, *persistence* is not the virtue of many people in the republic. It is common for a person to talk very emotionally about how s/he failed to achieve the expected results after investing time and resources into something and often s/he become an advocate of demotivating others from trying the same thing.

When thinking of the poor, women are more affected by poverty than men. It may be true that women are less genetically capable of performing some tasks than men. In contrast, women as much as men, are born equal in terms of creative thinking and intelligence. Spelke in 2005 documented that during infancy, boys and girls depict no or few differences in spatial or counting abilities evidencing that the differences may be occurring as they socialize with the people around them. As they grow up, gender roles,discrimination and social expectations, may be at play. We are now witnessing more women taking science subjects, entering politics and performing tasks that traditionally, were performed predominantly by men. As such, women are equally expected to have critical thinking skills as men. The common mistake of the poor is often to think that critical thinkers must always be men forgetting that women have an equally important role.

Another aspect of intelligence that is highly influenced by informal or traditional learning is the *interpersonal intelligence*; the capacity to understand emotions, intentions, motivations and desires of other people. Culture is an ultimate precursor of interpersonal intelligence. The poor are excellent in understanding the emotions, intentions, motivations and desires of the people who are very close or dear to them such as family, clan or tribesmen. However, their ability to understand the true intentions, motivations and desires of people who are not closely related to them is often limited. Most politicians for example, often manipulate the poor by hiding their true intentions, motivations and desires for political positions and expresses short lived emotions, intentions and desires by extending helping hands during political campaigns.

The interpersonal intelligence is often evident in terms of political allances the republic of the poor, however, failures are common. For example, these political alliances been established but often they are short lived. Political alliances may be considered as the relationship between different political entities or agents of political entities that is facilitated when each member of the alliance has a common interest and genuine intentions and open to other member's ideas and thoughts (interpersonal intelligence). Alliances are formed with the possibility that another member may become a leader and treats everyone with unconditional positive regard such as valuing members in the alliance whose entities may be less powerful in terms of number of members. This is often lacking in the alliances of in the republic.

I will avoid using the word mental retardation as one of my friends often describes the poor. Mental retardation is defined by Switzky and Greenspan (2006) as *the generalized disorder ascribed to people who have an IQ below seventy who have experienced deficits since childhood, and who have trouble with basic life skills such as dressing and feeding oneself and communicating with others.* Although most of the poor people meets at least fifty percent of the variables in this definition of mental retardation, such as, most scoring IQ less that seventy and have experienced socioeconomic deficits since childhood, classifying them as mentally retarded is quite extreme as almost all are capable of performing a full range of basic life skills. However, constant environmental-mediated socioeconomically deprivation (although some have linked poverty with genetics) has resulted into thinking capacities that lie at the lower margins of retardation. It is very common to see a physically capable individual sleeping in a house with a nearly falling roof while there is a forest full of trees just behind his compound. I think it is logical to classify this kind of person as mentally retarded.

It is also true that people in the republic have 'hidden' psychological disorders. A psychological disorder was defined by Butcher, Mineka and Hooley (2007) as an *on-going dysfunctional patterns of thought, emotion and behaviour that causes significant distress, and that is considered deviant in that person's culture of society.* Psychological or mental illnesses are very common and their impact is strong on people who are poorer, of low socioeconomic class, and from disadvantaged groups. However, due to strong interpersonal intelligence among poor people, the copying mechanisms for psychological conditions such as poverty mediated depression are diverse in their republic. In the rural areas of the republic for example, unlike the cities, a person who have nothing to eat may just knock on a neighbor's door during lunch time and would share whatever is available. However, these copying mechanisms does not always suppress outburst of behaviors associated with psychological conditions. Reports on a parent burning an offspring's hand for stealing few coins and other events of the sort are common due to *hidden* mental conditions in the republic.

Psychologists consider for a condition to be classified as a *physiological disorder*, it needs to have a significant impact on an individual's life in terms of distress and dysfunction. In this context, I consider inability to think critically as a mental dysfunction and a distress and have negative consequences to the people who depend on others such as children. Children are persistently dependent on their parents in terms of food, shelter, health and education until they attain the age that is socially considered as a time for them to be independent. Parents who cannot think critically to devise solutions that address the needs of their children, both immediate and long-term are dysfunctional and a distress, in economic context and can be considered technically as having psychological disorders in thinking.

I discussed the role of brain development in intelligence and critical thinking. Susser, Neugerbauer, Hock and colegues (1996) linked poverty, malnutrition and diseases to disruptions in normal brain development in infancy that are believed to cause schizophrenia, a mental disorder.

Poverty, malnutrition and non infectious diseases are ubiquitous in our republic.In the 2012 UNICEF report , about 67.9percent of the people in the republic lived below international poverty line of US$1.25 per day; this means more than 2/3 of the people in the republic are poor. The republic has only a 2.8percent public spending on health as a percent of GDP, thus the chances of controlling the diseases are slim. This means that a greater percentage of the people in the republic dwells within the schizophrenic risk zone and will continue to be there as long as the spending on health remains the same. It also means that the children born by these 2/3 of the people in the republic are at increased risk of schizophrenia.

There are many people in the republic showing different symptoms of depression such as feelings of helplessness and hopelessness, loss of interest in daily activities, feelings of worthlessness, loss of energy and increase in physical complaints. These symptoms may continue to silently enchain people in poverty limiting their creative thinking that is necessarily for moving out of the cycles of poverty. However, people in the republic may see this with a political lens linking this to poor governance and accountability among political leaders forgetting that the people need to be equally accountable for their life.

The followers of emotional intelligence school of thoughts believe that our thoughts are linked to our feelings and emotions which is a basic principle of the Cognitive Behaviour Therapy. It is believed that if someone is feeling depressed, the thoughts of sadness or hopelessness dwells in their mind and this may result into negative behaviors such as not working. It may results as well into choosing activities that may continue to impoverish an individual, hoping to relieve sadness or hopelessness. It is necessary therefore that when dealing with thoughts, we need as well to pay attentions to mental conditions that may cause depressive moods.

Mood disorders are very common in the republic although they may be silent. Several people may be *anhedonic*, meaning they cannot experience pleasure from activities usually found enjoyable by others such as working or exercise. There are many people with generalized anxiety disorders in which they are persistently worried about money, health, family life or their relations ending into dysfunction and distress. People who are excessively worried of these needs are willing to trade their rights such as votes for things like money, food or clothing regardless of the true intentions of the person that they give their votes to. These people may revert to alcoholism, as a way of clearing their thoughts and worries consequently using even a small amount of money that could have been used to meet family expenses further pushing themselves deeper and deeper in the ruins of poverty.

Excessive worries are part of what we call *conscious process.* Consciousness is a good thing because as long as you are conscious it simply means that you are connected to your environment. The consciousness I am referring to here is the type of consciousness that results from someone realizing that he is not living up to his goals or expectations. One of the weaknesses of the poor is that when he perceives that he is not or cannot (in his own definition) live up to his goals or expectations, he chooses behavior that aid an escape from that conscious thought instead of behaviors that would facilitate facing it. As such, he chooses, for example, to engage in alcohol or locally available psychoactive agents such as Marijuana as a way of escaping the conscious thoughts.

Psychologists in Charles Stangor (mentioned earlier) , suggests the use of behavioral and cognitive therapies in dealing with the disorders of the thought. Behaviour therapy is based on the principles of learning that encompasses operant conditioning by using rewards and punishment as well as observing positive behaviors of others.

Reinforcements is considered as the best option for teaching new skills, for example, paying handsomely for the crops of new graduates who decided to engage in faming soon after getting their university degrees. On the other hand, cognitive therapy that is aimed at helping the client to identify bad beliefs contributing to negative behaviour and helps people to develop new, healthier ways of thinking about themselves and others around them. Cognitive therapy aims at identifying the negative beliefs, challenging them and helping an individual to replace them with more rational ones :consequently developing more appropriate behaviors. One of the barriers of applying these approaches is that almost 70 percent of the people in the republic are poor and may be in need of these therapies that are more individualized andit may be impractical to manage all residents of the republic this way. Therefore, this discussion aims at coercing the *experts* to look at the problems of the republic as more psychological in the context of disordered thought than socio-economically, although the latter is equally important.

You have heard people talk about subconscious state. Joseph Murphy, a former fellow of the Andhra Research University of India wrote a book,*The Power of your Sub-Conscious Mind.* Even Sigmund Freud wrote a book in 1899 titled *The Interpretation of Dreams.* There are a lot of psychologists identifying themselves as psychoanalysts who have conducted massive research on subconscious state. In simple terms, the subconscious state is dominated by dreams. Dreams are defined by Stangor (2010) as *the successions of images, thoughts, sounds and emotions that pass through our minds while sleeping.* It's considered that, although people dream several times at night, a large percentage of our dreams are forgotten upon waking up.

My interest is the content of the dream itself. Cartwright and colleagues in 2006 reported that the content of our dreams is generally linked to our daily experiences, concerns, fears and failures. The environment we live in and our culture shapes our daily experiences, as such, people in different environments and cultures have different dreams. Different socio-economic environments also cause different dreams among different groups. For example, while a person in a wealthier environment might be having nightmares of armed robbery or happy moments by flying in airplane, a person in poor family might be having nightmares of witches entering the house or night-flying over his roof. This depicts how environment shape our dreams.

Based on this, it goes without saying that the content of dreams of the poor in the republic would always reflect the experiences, concerns, features and failures related to poverty such as dreaming of sickness, hunger, witchcraft and such like. Thus, to enhance the power of subconscious mind, the poor need to be filled with the thoughts and experiences that would promotes non-poverty dream contents. People whose dreams are filled with poverty related contents are more likely to have extremely poor critical thinking skills and judgements including interpretation or assigning values to their dreams in their daily life

In attempt to improve Critical thinking (and intelligence), scientists in earlier years have actually thought of crazy ideas such as *Eugenics*. Eugenics in this context is an attempt to improve human intelligence by encouraging marriage for the purpose of reproduction of only those people who are intelligent. This was very common in United States and even laws were passed to prevent entry into the countries of those people from countries marked by low intelligence.

Eugenics is not uncommon in our republics. Wealthier or educated families often prefer marrying their children to wealthier or highly educated families, likewise, poor families often desires marrying their children to wealthier or educated families. The Chagga and Kikuyu tribes are among the highly eugenic tribes. This , has made these tribes among the advantaged in terms of socio-economic indicators. As a result, the people in our republics have stereotyped these and the like minded tribes as pro-wealth.

Eugenics is not only limited to financial and academic excellence desires, but also to other characteristics such as avoidance of families with history of chronic diseases and witchcraft. In my village for example, chances of getting married were slim if born in a family painted as witches or with history of chronic diseases such as leprosy. Although scientists   call this stigma, it has possibly made them scientists, owing to the eugenic choices of their parents. The evidence of whether this approach is successful is compelling but mixed. The truth however remains that if the poor chooses to marry another of the same caliber for example, which is a common practice in our republic it is guaranteed that their children will also be poor. They can still turn the coin upside down if at least one of the poor partners is a critical thinker, that s/he possesses intelligence capacity beyond the margins of retardation and that has the ability to achieve academic and economic excellence beyond the cycles of poverty.

Critical thinking is also related to language skills. One thing for sure is that the republic may be poor economically but it very rich in languages. Republics in East Africa for example are among the countries with diverse cultures in terms of ethnic groups (Schmied,1982). Tanzania and Kenya consists of more than 120 and 70 ethnic groups respectively demonstrating uniquely diverse cultures. These ethnic groups are marked with distinct vernacular languages. Charles Stangor states that language allows access to existing knowledge, drawing important conclusions, setting and accomplishing goals, understanding and communicating in complex social relationships. Language is considered as one of the critical aspect of our ability to think without which, a human being would not have been as intelligent. Language is also one of the key distinctions between human being and animals. Unfortunately, the intelligence tests are often delivered in English which is considered as the global language. It is likely delivering the very same tests in national or tribal languages would yield different test results. Thus, perhaps to be intelligent in global context, it may be seen that understanding the 'global language' is a prerequisite. People in western countries have often attributed intelligence among Africans to the ability to speak English, presenting such a biased view on intelligence. This is evidenced by the fact that English language is often a requirement for scholarships or opportunities to study in the west.

Different language and contexts may have different characteristics attributed to intelligence. A Maasai youth, *Morani* who fights a lion may be regarded as intelligent in terms of learning the lion's movements and tricking into killing it. In our tribe for example, an intelligent person was the one who is able to memorize hearth-time stories told by grandmothers. All in all, intelligence in all these contexts encompasses *learning* (learning of lions movements as well as learning to memorize). Thus, language that creates opportunities for learning would definitely promote intelligence.

Language strongly influences human thought process. There is a concept called *linguistic relativity*. As described by Charles Stangor, this is an ideology that language and its structures influence and limit human thought. This is evidenced by an observation that one language may have many words for a situation or something while another language have relatively fewer words for the same thing and that this difference influences how people in these two languages perceive that situation. However, there are mixed views on whether language influences perception and thought as commented by Levinson (1998), since other researchers have documented contrary ideas to linguistic relativity. Even if it is unclear whether language influences our perceptions and thoughts, the importance of language in learning, which is a prerequisite to achieve expertise needed as one of the five components of creativity, is indispensable. Unfortunately, most of our traditional languages in the republic serves the purpose of interpersonal communications only and provides limited opportunities for learning.

Lack of vocabularies or even words for bigger words such as millions or billions is another setback in the learning process. The wealthy vernacular languages in the republics are less likely to be used for formal learning, as evidenced by no or few books in such languages. Thus, although the republic is rich in languages, the use of such languages for learning is limited. The national language on the other hand, forms an ultimate opportunity for learning at the national level. However, some of the poor have weak comprehension of the words in these languages, evidenced by the fact that when opposition politicians for example, explain issues such as corruption during electoral campaigns, the poor may not understand what they are talking about. Moreover, it has also been argued that people, who have a whole range of understanding of a common language, are equally intelligent. Therefore, to transform the poor, comprehension of language is a neccessity.

Language, both verbal and nonverbal, is a requirement for *learning* which entails a change in knowledge and behaviors resulting from observations we make throughout our life experiences. We learn how to breastfeed at earlier stages of life and slowly becoming independent, capable of finding food for ourselves in adulthood. Learning also involves acquiring skills to respond to changes in our environment. Stangor (2010) explains three aspects of learning namely *conditioning*, which is a type of behaviour programming that encompasses the ability to connect changes in our environment with responses to these changes; *insight,* that is the sudden understanding of the solution to a problem and *observational learning or modelling-* learning that occurs by observing others.

It is important to understand that conditioning, both classical and operant, is a good thing when it is *positive*, as it helps an individual to develop expectations preparing him for both good and bad events. However, *positive* conditioning in *negative* behaviors may further escalate the behaviors. For

41

example, if an alcoholic man who did not leave money at home for buying food, is given food upon coming back home, he will be conditioned to become a very irresponsible man, and he will choose activities that reinforce this behaviour. Likewise, people who are given money, alcohol, food or cloths during electoral campaigns will be conditioned to become individuals who would not exercise their right of voting for a suitable candidate unless they are offered these items, and they would always expect hand-outs during electoral campaigns. At the national level, the overreliance on external aid have conditioned the leaders and citizens of the republic to believe that the republic cannot survive without aid, as such, leaders and even citizens have developed begging behaviors that promotes that belief. Unfortunately, this behavior is passed on to their offspring.

Insightful learning on the other hand, occurs when we suddenly find a solution to a problem. In mathematics, for example, a person may figure out the formula unexpectedly. Poor people have poor insights as they have limited ability to figure out the solution to their problems suddenly. This has resulted into several incidences of poor judgements in situations that need a quick solution. Likewise, observational learning has become a common method of learning in the republic. This occurs when people learn by observing others. It is expected that this learning occurs without a leaner engaging in what the majority may consider as a risky or immoral behaviour. It is also called modelling. Learning by modelling is more impactful if we observe people who are higher in the hierarchy and is less impactful if we observe the behaviors of people who are lower in the hierarchy.

Parents contribute to modelling the behaviors of their children. A child growing with an abusive parent is more likely to become abusive in the future. However, the very same child is more likely to ignore, warn or punish a younger sibling if he or she observes an abusive behaviour, instead of learning the behaviour. Likewise, observational learning plays a key role in issues of national concern such as corruption. A civil worker who observes his or her superior taking bribes is more likely to engage in bribery in the future. However, the same worker is more likely to ignore, warn or punish a junior worker who engages in bribery instead of learning. It is very common for people to perform certain behaviors just because someone superior to them is doing or has done the same thing.

Observational learning is the key mechanism through which people of the public learn risky and immoral behaviors. The problem with observational learning is that, even a suspicion of the behaviour may be enough motivator for imitation although the actual 'observation' has not taken place or even just by imitating the behaviors of a third party. A woman may decide to become unfaithful just because of a feeling that her husband (the primary party) is unfaithful or because a friend (the third party) have dealt with the same kind of the problem in the same way. In the republic it is very common for someone to take a bribe just because of the feeling that the superior figure is taking it or because a colleague may have took it without negative consequences.

Another aspect of learning is memory defined by Stangor (2010) as *the ability to store and retrieve information* and cognition, *the ability to acquire and utilize such information.* Memory can be classified as *explicit* and *implicit* as well as *sensory, short-term* and *long term.* Although I won't dwell much on this aspect, it is important to understand that people in the republic have memory problems ranging from mild, moderate to severe. The most commonly affected is the type of explicit memory called *recall memory,* the ability of bringing information from the memory 'store' that has been previously remembered. Recall memory is a common problem among politicians in the republic. They would say something and manages to remember it for quite some time but forgetting it at the end of the day. It is also common among citizens of the republic, they can vote for someone and in the long run come to hold a memorable evidence that the true intentions of the voted leader was not people's development but forgets about it when in such a position that requires him to make similar decision.

The politicians often manipulates people's memory by what I call *masking* of memorable events. Masking of memory occurs when there is a detrimental event in the republic and as long as the public keeps talking about it there is a real or perceived loss to the party involved, as such, another event is strategically designed to mask the thoughts of the people consequently shifting the discussion to the new event. A person whose memory is easily masked by events tends to quickly forget the critical events and focus on the non-critical ones. These people are technically transformed into powerless individuals who will no longer question their leaders.

Powerlessness makes someone, as Hobbes puts it; consent voluntarily to surrender some of his rights to the authorities in order to protect some of the remaining rights. In case of strike for example, a person who goes back to work in response to government's threat of dismissal, surrenders his rights to question that authority to protect the remaining right that is his salary! He surrenders his rights of earning a just and fair salary and healthier working environment to protect his right as a bread earner for the family. This kind of person will most likely not promote authority or status quo questioning behaviors among his children at home creating a complete cycle of young and adult members of the republic of the poor who cannot question the authorities.

Powerless people resort to blame and makes blaming an enjoyable game particularly when they talk among themselves as they are fearful of raising their voice to the authorities. They would blame other people for their failures. They would blame the governments for their inadequate housing, the state of their children's shirts and their poverty. In my opinion, the authorities should only play a greater role in designing mechanisms for the people to use their potential. The government's role is putting in place the economic and social infrastructures such as schools with enough teachers and books for the children to express their potential through education, markets for farming products and so on. However the responsibility of expressing your potential and pursuing your dream lies within yourself. Henry T. Hamblin in his books, *within you is power* and *the power of thought* comments that "man possesses illimitable powers within him. In most people, this power lies dormant and is hidden within man until is sufficiently evolved and unfolded [when he becomes] entrusted with its use. *Thought* is the greatest weapon in connecting man to his powers inside him".

To empower people does not mean provision of basic material needs just to make them feel truly a part of the greater society . It's all about helping them to reduce the poverty of the thought so that they can be able to show their potential. Again, Henry T Hamblin in *within you is power* continues that man has to become changed within himself before his life, in this context, poverty can be altered. He must change his ideas, his thoughts and his attitudes towards life and become transformed. When this change has been affected; he not only begins to repair his present life but he creates a finer and nobler life for the future and several generations to come. At this stage, such a man would become powerful enough to demand for quality of services, competences and accountability among his leaders without fear.

Further Reading

1. Bellinger, D. C., & Needleman, H. L. Intellectual impairment and blood lead levels [Letter to the editor]. The New England Journal of Medicine, 2003. 349(5), 500.
2. Brooks-Gunn, J., & Duncan, G. J. The effects of poverty on children. The Future of Children, 1997. 7(2), 55–71.
3. Butcher, J., Mineka, S., & Hooley, J. Abnormal psychology and modern life (13th ed.). Boston, MA: Allyn & Bacon.2007.
4. Cartwright, R., Agargun, M., Kirkby, J., & Friedman, J. Relation of dreams to waking concerns. Psychiatry Research, 2006.141(3), 261–270.
5. Ceci, S. J. How much does schooling influence general intelligence and its cognitive components? A reassessment of the evidence. Developmental Psychology, 1991.27(5), 703–722.
6. Charles Stangor. Introduction to Psychology. Flatworld Knowledge.2010.
7. Garlick, Integrating brain science research with intelligence research. Current Directions in Psychological Science, 2003.12(5), 185–189.
8. How to open the Door to your future. Open Colleges.2011.
9. Henry T. Hamblin. Within you is Power. CruGuru.2010
10. Henry T. Hamblin. The Power of Thought. CruGuru.2008
11. Kahabi G. Isangula. A Leaking Needle. CreateSpace.2011.
12. Levinson, S. C. Studying spatial conceptualization across cultures: Anthropology and cognitive science. Ethos, 1998. 26(1), 7–24.
13. McDaniel, M. A. Big-brained people are smarter: A meta-analysis of the relationship between in vivo brain volume and intelligence. Intelligence, 2005. 33(4), 337–346.
14. R. J. Sternberg (Ed.), Handbook of intelligence (pp. 396–420). New York, NY: Cambridge University Press.
15. Seagoe, M. V. Terman and the gifted. Los Altos, CA: William Kaufmann.1975.
16. Schmied, J.J. Edgar C. Polomé / C. P. Hill, eds., Language in Tanzania. English World-Wide, 1982. 3, 2.p257–260.
17. Spelke, E. S. Sex differences in intrinsic aptitude for mathematics and science? A critical review. American Psychologist, 2005. 60(9), 950–958.

18. Switzky, H. N., & Greenspan, S. What is mental retardation? Ideas for an evolving disability in the 21st century. Washington, DC: American Association on Mental Retardation.2006.

19. Susser, E. B., Neugebauer, R., Hock, H.W., Brown, A. S., Lin, S., Labowitz, D., & Gorman, J. M. Schizophrenia after prenatal famine: Further evidence. .Archives of general psychiatry, 1996.53, 25–31

20. Tarasova, I. V., Volf, N. V., & Razoumnikova, O. M. Parameters of cortical interactions in subjects with high and low levels of verbal creativity. Human Physiology, 2010. 36(1), 80–85.

21. Terman, L. M., & Oden, M. H. Genetic studies of genius: The gifted group at midlife (Vol. 5). Stanford, CA: Stanford University Press.1959.

22. Thomas Hobbes. The Leviathan. Chapter XIII: Of the Natural Condition of Mankind as concerning their felicity and misery. 1651.

23. Vibeke Venema.The Indian sanitary pad revolutionary. BBC World Service. 2014, March, 4th.

LESSON THREE

The Poor.
Dwellers of the City.

Eagles with no talons,
Wings without coverts,
Birds with no beaks,
Chickens without gizzards,
Nectars with no sugars,
Filaments without anters,
Hairs with no follicles,
Nails without lunulae,
Dwellers of the city!

The dwellers of the city is another group of the poor in our republic, the urban poor. There are several classes of this group. There are those who live in slum-like shelters, sharing a room with their children, shared public toilets and bathrooms. This group constitutes the majority of the dwellers of the city and retains the rural-like life style-supporting one another both economically and emotionally due to strong social cohesion. The only difference with the rural poor is that this class is at least exposed to modern lifestyle outside their dwellings-public transport, tarmacked roads, strong phone signals, automated teller machines, shopping malls etc. Most of members of this class do not always want to go back to rural areas, only visiting (in)frequently, as they become acculturated with urban life to the extent that the environment in their villages of origin becomes unbearable.

This class has the greatest impact on urban population due to their direct and indirect actions. Directly through poor family planning methods and utilization, perhaps due to retaining some attitudes and beliefs of the rural culture, strong social interactions that result into propagated sexual activities, lack of or premature termination of education due to social factors and so on. They also pull relatives or friends from rural areas to 'help' them find better lives in the city. This is because desires for economic wellbeing constitute the major reason for rural-urban migration as per Adamu Mustapha's article (2009), Michael Lipton (1980) and Gibson and Gurmu (2012). The assumption is that, one member of the family creates opportunities for others to move out the rural areas influencing the decisions to migrate. Moreover, the urban poor influence population growth indirectly through their actions when they visit the villages. Since most of them have what I call *unjust employments* (I will explain in the coming lesson), they have a flexible and relaxed schedule that allows them to visit their village more often compared to those with formal employments that require bureaucratic process of leave requests. These people often make savings of their income for a long period. When visiting rural villages, they would always buy nice cloths and lots of hand-outs for their relatives in advance. Upon arrival in the villages, their appearance and handouts creates a positive impression among the rural poor who might in turn wish to come to the city for better life.

Young girls are often tricked to come to the city as housemaids, barmaids, shop keepers, and wives. When traveling in a public transport in a republic one day, I overheard one young man complaining that his wife had left him after only eight months of marriage. The story caught my ears such that I continued with the journey despite arriving at my destination. He came to the city five years ago and faced a lot of hardships. He then started selling bottled water that earned about two dollars a day and was able to buy a bed and mattress and other items which to him, was a progress. He secured a low rent room in a semi-finished house in the city and decided to travel back to his village, utilizing one year's savings, in search of the love of his life. There was this beautiful lady who many young men of his age considered 'hard' to get. When this young man arrived in the village wearing new jeans, having a modern mobile phone and even new haircut, every girl was dying to be with him. As a result, he did not invest much efforts in finally 'marrying' this beautiful lady by the deceit of his appearance that signaled better life in the city.

They started the journey back to the city first using a bicycle from the village to the bus station that took them to the train station. The train was the only efficient and affordable model of transport to the city in the republic during that time. They arrived at the central railway station at midnight and the girl was amazed to see the traffic lights and skyscrapers. They took a bus then a motorcycle commonly known as Boda Boda navigating through narrow streets to their house. After four months of 'happy' marriage, the wife started changing her behavior according to this young man. She started spending most of her time outdoors often coming back home drunk. After eight months, the wife left and became a sex worker.

I was intrigued to follow up this story just to get to the core of it. I wanted to understand why she would leave this young man who had 'pulled' her from the village to the city. Unfortunately, I was unlucky. I can only speculate that perhaps this woman's impression of the better life that was depicted by this man when they first met in the village was not the same after arriving in the city. Perhaps she stuck with him for eight months just to learn her way out of the imprisonenment and since she couldn't find a better alternative, sex work was a choice.

The urban poor are also very distant to the middle class or high class in terms of income. There are physical and geographical barriers between these classes. Even the names that are assigned to this class' dwellings often reflect their level of economies. They are always traditional names that can be traced back to the disadvantaged situations. The names are like *Kibera* (Kenya), *Makoko* (Nigeria), *Kinawataka* (Uganda) or *Kigogo,* or *Manzese* (Tanzania) just to mention a few,. In contrast,the names of the well-off neighbourhoods usually have western names such as Beach, Bay, West or Estate. Even the roads in the poor dwellings have the names that reflects their economic status such as *Makoroboi* or *Makorokocho*, unlike in the rich's neighborhoods that the word 'road' is often replaced with '*drive'*.

City poverty runs in a vicious cycle within poor families. Most of the city poor will end up marrying their counterparts, increasing the likelihood of their children to become poor. Most often, one parent becomes a sole provider for the family whiles the other, often the woman, remains at home to look after children. The poor are often,technically not 'allowed' to date the rich , reflecting eugenicist. If it happens, it is mostly a sexual transaction and it could be against their will. The male poor, if unmarried and young often called *Serengeti boy*s in one of the republics are often compensated in exchange for the sexual services with older,richer women porpularly known as *sugar mummies*-this is a type of male sex work that has not been well documented. On the other hand, when the rich men find the poor girls attractive, they would invest a lot- renting her a house often in middle income dwellings, smart phones, and other necessities in exchange for sexual satisfaction. This kind of transactional sex has been receiving recognition in scholarly world with the rich men

51

often referred to as *'Buzi'* equivalent to a sexually mature male goat (buck). This is some sort of win-win situation that, while the Serengeti boys enjoys taste the good life with rich men's wives, who in turn gets sexual satisfaction; at the same time, the rich men enjoys sexual satisfaction with the sisters of Serengeti boys who in turn tastes the good life.

One time, I was traveling with a friend in one of the central regions in one of the republics. When having dinner in one of the hotels, a young beautiful girl came to sit near our table. My friend exchanged few words with her for about half an hour. Suddenly, a very senior member of the parliament,who is married with grandchildren, approached where we were sitting and the young girl jumped to kiss him daringly. They left in a government vehicle. The male hotel waiter approached us and explained the girl *belongs* to that 'honorable' man and he has invested a lot in her-renting her an apartment and a nice car . He further explained that if the man finds you talking to her, he can make you disappear indefinitely. It was my friend's lucky day as he still lives, perhaps the honorable did not take note of him. Often this kind of interactions between the poor and the rich and sometimes, the middle class and the poor contributes to unintended consequences or what I called mobile juniors (Isangula,2012). This results when the girl becomes pregnant and due to a need to maintain a good social status, the rich may distant himself, leaving the girl to deal with the consequences on her own. The good thing about the poor in our republic and so many others of the sort is that these kinds of immoral behaviors are highly tolerated. They would actually consider this as a sign of manhood and will never dare question or expose these acts even if the one involved is their elected leader. When these behaviors are questioned, the leaders or the rich would invest excessive efforts to mask them.

The poor in the city are very hard workers, although the earnings are not in synchronicity with their efforts. Women in particular are excessively hard workers-we see them in public transport carrying buckets of fresh or fried fish and baskets of tomatoes, onions and bananas so that they can earn to propagate their families. These are the ones making tasteful chapattis and andazis, even fried chips from sweet potatoes and cassava. They are the ones who sell every part of chicken-fried liver, intestines, legs, beaks and the head-everything except the feathers. Even those who work as housemaids, office cleaners or road sweepers are poorly paid and weakly protected in terms of occupational hazards, physical and emotional abuses and other dangers.

Some of the city poor, unlike their rural counterparts often understand the importance of education as a vehicle to strengthen the thoughts of their children. They struggle to send their children to schools. Their children however do not always reward their parents' efforts and tend to drop out or persist to the end with poor academic performances. The city poor often manage to build low quality houses after a lot of struggle and prolonged savings, when that happens the houses are neither designed by engineers nor built in planned areas of the city. They often the first to lose their home and belongings when flooding occurs or the city plans for things like road expansion.

The same kind of poor often equate being white as being rich. Whenever the white man *'mzungu'* visits some of the republics, particularly when volunteering, some of the poor will always befriend them with hidden expectations. I do however agree that the mzungus are naturally well received by the poor because of their strong *'welcoming'* culture, but most of them would always think of financial gain. Girls are struggling to have white boyfriends regardless of the fact that some of these *voluntourists* often comes to the republic under some sort of travel support grants. Voluntouristic girls are also often attracted to the poor. Sex tourism is very common in touristic areas of the republic. There have been documentations where girls or women have left their boyfriends or husbands for the energetic Maasai or found what they proclaim to be love in the republic as narrated in the *White Maasai* movie and several blog articles - Anuraag Sanghi (2012), Laprincessa (2013).

The poor, particularly most of the city poor are often forgetful; if one transcends from poor to rich status, only a few will look back to uplift others to where they are. Even those girls who have been left to care for the children alone after being pregnant by the rich men (the Buzis), often forget and repeat the same mistake. When they earn money and transtition from poor to middle class, they would always form a strong association with the rich, often forgetting their humble background. Although this is a good strategy for success,in financial terms-the power of positive associations-but 'forgetting' here means how they fail to inspire and support others to come out of poverty.

Further Reading

1. Adamu Mustapha. The impact of rural-urban migration on the economy of rural areas in Wudil local government area of Kano state Nigeria. Techno Science Africana Journal.2009; Vol.3:1.

2. Anuraag Sanghi. Zanzibar: Where women come to buy sex. Available at
   http://quicktake.wordpress.com/2012/02/12/zanzibar-where-women-come-to-buy-sex/

3. Isangula, K.G. Mobile juniors: Street Children, Orphanhood and Child Development. Law & Psychology eJournal. 2012. Vol 6, Issue 2.

4. Laprincessa. Sex Tourism in Tanzania. Available at
   http://laprincessaworld.blogspot.com/2013/02/sex-tourism-in-zanzibar.html

5. Michael Lipton.Migration from rural areas of poor countries: The impact on rural productivity and income distribution.
   World Development.1980.Vol.8,1;1–24.

LESSON FOUR

The Poor.
The Servants of the Republic.

Poverty is rich, in kindness and comfort
A fairy tale, of struggle in quests
Harmless it sound, harmful in verily
An outlaw, in the court of the haves,

There is another group of the poor in the republic-the civil servants, who mostly fall within the middle class. This group includes teachers, doctors, nurses, armed forces, engineers and any civil worker you know. Before I proceed, let me tell you a story of my father and myself,though at first the story seems somewhow unrelated to the topic at hand.

My father was never a civil servant, perhaps because he never excelled in schools. He worked in a private ginnery for few years to raise capital for his fishing business. For some time, the fishing business worked quite well for him. We enjoyed our childhood for a short period before everything changed suddenly. The only development he could make from his business was marrying a second wife and going far away from my village to one of the island in the republic where fishing activities were pronounced. We found ourselves turning into a single mom system within a polygamist marriage. There was a time when we thought our father was dead as we couldn't communicate with him for several years and my mother became both a father and a mother. Her tireless struggles, often selling the illegal local brews and cigars , helped me and my young brother to reach to a secondary school. During schooling, I walked in my father's footsteps often considering fishing as a carreer . Fishing during school breaks, selling dried cassava plus my mother's contribution facilitated my fees to a high school. At the time, it was a high school for the so called 'special' students who performed well in secondary schools. In the final year at the high school, I started getting sick from unknown disease. Surprisingly, the disease was relieved whenever I went back to my village. The poor citizens started linking this with witchcraft because I was the only one from my village who escalated to the high school among my age mates. I was made to hold a spear on the cemetery of the great grandfather who I was named after. All these attempts did not bear fruits.

At a personal level, I never believed on the dead controlling my destiny. Dead souls are dead and if we mingle on their souls to control our destiny, we become the living dead in our minds and thoughts. I believed this to be biological rather than spiritual. It turned out that I was right as I was later diagnosed at the National hospital with a curable condition. Knowing the cause is always the first step in solving a problem and I was able to control my disease.

I later joined a medical school. During our time, only those who performed well in high school pursued courses such as medicine and engineering. Aftermedical school, I was supposed to choose between working as a civil servant or work for non-profit organization. Everyone advised me to go for a public sector and were against the not for profit sector. The public service was hailed for its job security and pension payments. My father, who resurfaced as a poor citizen , strongly encouraged me to go for a job in civil service. His arguments were, like many others; job security, big retirement packages, chances to help him and other villagers when they come to my hospital and perhaps one day, I may be appointed as a district medical officer.

I told you this story because these are the reasons for most of the poor civil servants to stick to their jobs; job security, big retirement packages and expectations of being appointed to be in charge of a certain unit, department or directorate. For me, these were no strong motives. I preferred a job with risks that will challenge my thoughts and beliefs. I wanted a job that will allow me to excel career-wise as a result of my performance, not as a result of someone's grace.

My definition of 'poor civil servants' inferred here is those afraid of taking risks; those who start worrying about retirement packages from day one of their first employment. Those who do not wish to see their dependents face any difficulty even for a single day. Those who cannot invest time or other resources into endeavors that seems to be risker. I envy them for their dedication to their families even if it means just working for *survival* with no progress. To them, salary is everything even if it means poor working conditions, poor performance management systems and so on. After sometime, when the social and family demands exceed the salary earned, the poor servants will embark on other easy means such as corruptions to meet the immediate needs. They will seize any opportunity for 'petty corruption' as Judge Warioba calls it in his 1995 corruption report presented by Edward Hoseah (2001) and also described by Afrobarometer (2006a & 2006b), Claude Ake (1993), Kamuzora (2004 & 2005) and Mekuila (2000). The petty corruption however, is not a guarantee for civil servants to meeting all of their immediate needs as such; they may become trapped in the ruins of poverty.

The petty corruptions affect the poor citizens, both the poor rural and the city poor equally. Since this form of corruption affect the poor directly in the course of seeking services such as legal or medical (Isangula, 2012); it is always used as a decoy for grand corruption. The corruption agencies in the republics may dwell on addressing petty corruption because it affect citizens directly at an individual level, while investing fewer efforts on grand corruption whose effect may not be immediately seen at the individual level. The authority may intervene by transferring servants involved or terminating their contracts(rarely); consequently, the poor will be happy and fall in love with the authority. Here, we learn that if matters that affects the poor directly are addressed, the poor will hail the intervening authority, turning a blind eye to the same matter that does not affect them directly or in the short term.Grand corruption, although it does not affect the poor directly, it does so indirectly through slowing macro development and increasingthe cost of living.

Salary is everything to the poor servants. They would do anything to keep receiving their salaries, even if the salary is so small that it entraps them in situational poverty. Often, they may join movements that support remuneration increments. Although the core aim of these movements may be to improve living situations (Isangula 2012), the entrapped servants will always talk of remuneration increase. When threatened that what they are receiving now may be discontinued and that they may be fired, they would return to work - because salary caters for their immediate needs. In Isangula (2012), the Tanzanian Medical Doctors' strike had two concerns, namely; the working conditions of the doctors, including infrastructure, drug availability, equipment and other medical supplies, and underpayment in terms of salaries and allowances. The strike ended prematurely after the authority threatened to terminate all the doctors who were involved if they did not report back to work within a set deadline.

Likewise, the workers unions for the poor servants are also poor. Since the leaders of these unions come from the same pond- they are easily sold out. The unions will make a lot of noise over remuneration and better working conditions, but, the authority buys them out very easily. It is like the poor activists- those whose personal gain in terms of finance and fame is important than the majority gains (Isangula, 2012b). The unions of the poor servants become castrated to stand for the poor.

As I said earlier, most of the poor servants are pro salaries regardless of the quality of services that they offer. They are more likely to stop giving a certain service if one of the items needed to offer that service is absent or dysfunctional. Instead of creatively looking for solutions using both divergent and convergent thinking.They are more liley to wait for the authority to prescribe a solution. A teacher, for example, is more likely to stop teaching because there are no chalks or the writing board is damaged until the authority solves the problem. A laboratory scientist is more likely to stay idle in the laboratory since the machine is dysfunctional instead of looking for a solution. A nurse is more likely to stop conducting delivery because there is no light instead of looking for a solution. A policeman is more likely stop recording your complaints because there are no papers instead of solving the problem. They became like students in public schools who celebrates the power-cut even if the examination is in the next day. Or those students who let themselves fail the exams because their father will send them to universities eitherway. It is like a horse that would not turn until the owner hits it or a car that would not start unless pushed.

Most of the poor servants are afraid of reading to advance their careers which is one of the sustainability needs and often puts the personal gain ahead of knowledge gain. They usually prefer paid seminars and workshops and after the workshop, they would request for refresher trainings in the feedback forms before even applying the knowledge they have acquired. This has been a common recommendation among the trainees I have personally trained. Often, the requests for the refresher trainings are not because they want to gain knowledge, rather the financial gain associated with these trainings are the principal motive. Most often, they would ask when the next training is whenever you meet. One of my friends was annoyed by a poor servant who inquired when the next training would be conducted so that he could buy iron roofing sheets for his house because the initial training helped him to build the wall. These kinds of poor servants would always decay their knowledge exponentially as they focus more on personal financial gain to address immediate needs rather than career growth.

I must however appreciate that there are some of the servants who have good analytical and critical thinking skills, those who are pro-excellence, pro-perfection and pro-quality. Unfortunately, most of the institutional frameworks in the republic are often poor and do not protect, carter and nurture these servant's excellence. They are often seen as barriers or threats to other (senior) poor servants' efforts towards financial gain and may be called different names by their colleagues because they are strict on procedures. One of my friends has been in the public service for some years and has faced a lot of obstacles just because perfection is a key driver in his work. As an accountant, he has been refusing kickbacks from suppliers and always insisting of adhering to public procurement Act. Suprisingly, he has been investigated for corruption in several occasions simply because he refused to authorize a financial deal that did not adhere to procurement procedures within his unit. He has continued to innovatively handle his work pressures to the extent that no one has actually succeeded in breaking him despite several instances in which he was threatened.

These are the kinds of civil servants we need in our republics.

Further Reading

1. Afrobarometer. Combating Corruption in Tanzania: Perception and Experience.Afrobarometer Briefing Paper No. 33. AFROBAROMETER and REPOA.2006a.

2. Afrobarometer.Delivery of Social Services on Mainland Tanzania: Are People Satisfied?" Afrobarometer Briefing Paper No. 34. AFROBAROMETER and REPOA. 2006b.

3. Claude Ake. Deeper into Original Sin: The Context of the Ethical Crisis in Africa's Public Sevices." Chapter 2 in Rasheed Sadig and Dele Olowu (Eds.)Ethics and Accountability in African Public Services. United Nations Economic Foundation

for Africa and Africa Association for Public Administration and Management. ICIPE Science Press. 1993.

4. Edward G. Hoseah.PLENARY 3: Measures to combat Corruption at the Local, National and International Level.Paper presented at the 15th International Conference on Politics, Crime and Criminal Justice, Organized by the International Society for the Reform of Criminal Law, Canberra, Australia, 26-30 August 2001.

5. Isangula, K, G. Activism during Doctor's Strike in Tanzania, Success and Setbacks. Labor: Personnel Economics eJournal. 2012. Vol. 4, Issue 12. 2012.

6. Isangula, K, G. Viewpoint: Moral and Ethical Dilemmas During Medical Doctor's Strike in Tanzania. Negotiation Processes & Communications eJournal. 2012. Vol. 4, Issue 12.

7. Isangula, KG. A Leaking Needle (Sindano Inayovuja), a comprehensive review of Opportunities for Corruption in Health   Sector in Tanzania and Solutions. Createspace Publishing. 2012.

8. Peter Kamuzora. Socio – economic Context of Ethics in Health Care: A Case Study of Corruption in Public Health Systems in Tanzania. Tanzania Journal of Development Studies, 2004. 5 (2): 33 – 51.

9. Kamuzora, Peter.Strategies for Public Sector Corruption Prevention. Experience from Public Health Systems in Tanzania.Tanzania Journal of Development Studies, 2004.5 (2): 33 – 51.

10. Makeula, D.Factors Influencing Corruption in Health Services Delivery. Proceedings of the 18th TPHA Scientific Conference. Tanzania Public Health Association, Dar es Salaam.2000.

The Poor.
The Inventors of Decorations.

Welcome to the kingdom, of love and needs.
Where we dance and sing, songs of the dead.
Dwelling of the precious, a jewelry's' nest.
We whistle our cries, in the ears of the deaf.
A land of trees, a land of thousand wonders.
A republic, of Inventors of Decorations!

A friend visiting my house from abroad was amazed by a chandcraft in my sitting room; a cup like tool that has a 30-centimeter stick or you may call it a handle, decorated by markings that were locally imprinted using fire. While this craft was in my sitting room as a decoration, one or several tribes in the rural parts of the republic   were using the same tool as a cup for drinking water and local brews. Perhaps someone had invented this item when the community was faced with problems that created a need for a cup with an extended handle for drinking fluids in the village. My guess is, perhalps the initial design had no handle and after experimenting for several years, the inventor or others after him might have realized that a much longer handle was needed, consequently attaching to it a stick that is about 30 centimeters long, so that people would not contaminate the pots when taking waters and local brews. Perhaps, the tribe had witnessed deaths from outbreaks of contamination related diseases such as diarrhoea that was linked to cups with short or no handles. These are just my speculations.

To understand innovation, let us see difference between invention, innovation and improvement as described in the Management Sciences for Health's participants handbook on the Business planning for Health published in 2013. An *invention* is something that has never been seen before; it represents an attempt by the idea initiator or an inventor to meet an immediate need that is not yet met in the society, as per this lesson's context. Here, the key driver of invention is the *immediate need* or problem in the society and that the inventor comes up with a new solution to address the need. The so called poor families have invented thousands of items or tools to help them address their immediate needs. From the so-called stone ages, human beings were inventing regardless of their level of development or resources.

Human history books and evolution evidences (Jenny, 2012) , Bamber Gascoigne (History World) and many other historians, have documented inventions of fire, housing, stone made spears, knives and so many items during stone ages. These books and articles have described the use of rocks that carried a specific shape depending on the immediate need it was invented for. If the need was the roots that were the major sources of food and medicines, a rock was sharpened to facilitate digging of the roots so does the round-shaped stones for grinding cereals. In my village for example, before introduction of milling machines, until 90's we used to have two rounded stones- a small and bigger one. The small stone, *ensagbo*, was used to squeeze cereals such as millet against large stones to make flour that would later be used for making meals. Also, for materials that were non-squeezable such as pieces of cassava, a special designed piece of wood, *ehore* was used by women to grind dried pieces

63

between their legs on a large stone ,making cassava flour that was the main staple food.. These inventions are still used in villages where the milling machines are not available and we may be intrigued to say that these people are still trapped in the Stone Age.

During the Iron Age, the inventions were revolutionized and people designed iron melting techniques that resulted into improved farming tools, hunting tools even tools used in wars between clans or kings. The use of spears,shields,archery and other inventions in the Maji Maji war led by Kinjekitile Ngwale in Southern Tanzania and other anti-colonialism movements in the dark continent has been well documented in Godfrey Mwakikagile (2000), Richard Petraitis and John Iliffe (1979), Adu Boahen (1990) andBasil Davidson (1969) just to cite a few.These documented inventions, do not however, mean that people were not inventing before this.

On the other hand, *innovation*, according to the Management Sciences for Health book is when an invention moves from the hands of an inventor to the production line of a manufacturing plant, so that the masses can have access to the good or items. This simply means mass production of invented items to address the need of a diverse population group. The mass use of inventions I described above, for example,in wars or food processing generally entails innovation. Other examples would be if the country had no cups or if there were an outbreak of cholera that created a huge demand for cups of the same design as the one I described above;someone would have decided to take the invention from the hand of the inventor to mass produce the cups and perhaps export to other countries. Most of the inventions slowly progressed into innovation, however, in conventional thinking, innovation is often considered in industrial terms. During Kinje Kitile era, for example, micro industries were established to mass produce the spears,archery and shields to supply the army with tools for the war against colonialists. There are massive evidences of inter-tribe businesses during pre-colonial era (Eades, 1980), meaning these items that were traded and therefore, met the criteria for innovations.

Likewise, *improvement* entails an incremental change to an innovation that retains the integrity of the product, but improves its features or functionality. In this context, it means that the cup is modified to fit the need of different people. If someone has no hand to hold the handle- a rope can be added so that the cup can be hanged on the neck or something like that. The documented inventions and innovations were modified from time to time to meet the need of different people or groups within and beyond the societies.

Most of you would agree with me when I say that the level of inventions or innovation has slowed significantly in our republics compared to the western countries. There are several factors that have contributed over time to masking the ability of people particularly in developing countries to invent and innovate. Colonialism, western education, individualism and free market that have made Africans more of consumers than producers are among the few contributing factors..

During the anti-colonialism movements, most of the inventions such as spears and shields failed to withstand the guns of the colonialists. When the colonialists came into power, guns replaced most of the local inventions and even those people who continued to invent were silenced due to fear of a coup. Also, colonialism resulted into change in lifestyle from traditional ways of living to modernized life styles that translated into impregnated inventions in African societies. The 'natural' challenges faced by people that inspired inventions to address societal needs changed to human-made challenges that only focused on addressing the needs of the colonial masters. These were accompanied by introduction of prescribed inventions to the colonized people and the   slaves did not have a choice but to use them.

Colonialism also introduced a formal education,   the

65

education of the so called civilized. The type of education that my friend in Uganda, Gerald Otim, a co-founder of *Ensibuuko* describes as the one that 'does not promote experience-based learning' rather instructor- depended. Students are taught by instructors who are believed to be intelligent than them at a time, to answer questions in the exams but not solving the real life challenges. Earlier, I gave an example of an art teacher in elementary school who would score me lower marks for designing handmade items such as wooden spears or knives in art assignments, at the same time giving higher marks for students who would submit industrial made items such plastic cups or plates that they have bought from shops. Western education has continued programming students to become non inventors and consumers of technologies that have not sufficiently met the basic needs, particularly in poor communities. These students, because they are trained to consume modern technologies rather than inventing, would consequently become what I call *'technoslaves'*. They prefer living in areas where they have opportunities to enjoy these modern technologies, mostly, urban areas. Transport and communication infrastructures are more advanced in urban areas; as a result, the technoslaves will not enjoy life in rural areas where they would face 'real' life challenges. These slaves have no sufficient skills to neither use the technology to solve the challenges in rural communities nor can they design alternative solutions.This is illustrated by a friend who returned to the city only a day after visiting his parents in the village. His children, so addicted to electricity in the city, were unable sleep because the locally made light source gave them nightmares including seeing the house being on fire. This friend of mine could have explored the environment, partly using the available resources and applying his formal skills and perhaps technology, to solve the light challenge in the village instead of running away. As a result of all these deficiencies, in the long run, particularly after colonialism, all the invention attempts changed into historical handcrafts that are now used as decorations instead of addressing social needs. The potential inventors are now making handcrafts for decorative purposes.

I am not against technologies ,of course, I am a consumer and perhalps one of technoslaves, however, my argument is that formal education in the republic should create opportunity for people to invent solutions to their contextualized social needs rather than nurturing them to become consumers of the western technologies. Our capacity to equate with the western world in terms of technology is far beyond reach, thus, we need to start from what we have and what we are good at. We are mostly still in what Anthony Giddens (1990) calls the pre-modern society in his book *the consequences of modernity*. We need context based inventions that will address the republic's basic needs particularly at the lowest level. I would be happy to see that the inventions are transformed from historical handcrafts that are used as decorations to items that are addressing social needs.

Individualism has also contributed to masking invention capabilities. In the Stone and Iron Ages, people were mostly focusing on addressing societal needs. Primitive communalism, that is somehow still depicted in rural areas of our republics, promoted societal life in which there was a collective responsibility in addressing societal needs. Modern life has resulted into disintegration of this and people are now focusing on addressing individual rather than societal needs. We talk of personal development, personal success, personal health, personal car etc . Most of the revolutionary technologies are focusing on addressing personal needs. Since inventions aim at solving societal or community problems, a focus on individual needs offers no opportunity to invent but on consuming or improving the ready-made or imported inventions.

Free market economy coupled with higher imports of modern inventions and less exports of local inventions has made people weak inventors. The 'modern era' person is forced to consume 'modern era inventions' in solving local problems as such, the word 'consumer' have become synonymous with 'inventor'. People in the republic are struggling to *invent modern inventions* by exploring what is 'new' in the west so that they can become the first to use them. People in the republic are struggling to *invent* the latest smart phones or tablets by becoming the first to own them. If you visit a friend and find that he has a new brand of the car, then you will start saving money so that the next month or year you buy a similar car or a latest model to solve your transport problem. We are programmed to live a formal life- buying pre-manufactured cars for travelling to work, use pre manufactured TVs, rice cookers, fridges, sofas and so on- things we never invented. And the good thing is, we don't even bother to read the user manuals that could have opened our eyes how these items are operating and often we misuse them. It should be remembered that invention is all about asking ourselves questions for whatever we see. Asking ourselves for example why would a mango fall from a tree where there is no strong wind, instead of just enjoying the free meal.

Several years back, the former South African president Thabo Mbeki discouraged the distribution of AIDS drugs for use in public hospitals in order to further explore the reasons behind the African AIDS epidemic. This was an attempt to analyze a social problem that could have resulted into an invention to address it. However, activists, scientists and European and North American governments were not happy with this- it simply means if Mbeki's efforts were successful in *inventing* a contextualized solution to AIDS, western pharmaceuticals would not sell the anti-retroviral drugs to South Africa. In 2000, Mbeki invited dissidents and conventional scientists to discuss issues concerning AIDS, specifically interested to find out why the virus behaved differently in Africa compared to the West. His aspiration was to find an African interpretation and solution to the African problem. The west and American medias such as BBC News, the Guardians and others, did not take these efforts positively since they were offended bythe fact that an African dared to form his own opinion on what the American and European Scientists had already defined and prescribed Antiretroviral drugs and condoms, all supplied by them as a solution (Martin Asser 2000a & 2000b).

The media started propaganda with the intentions of portraying Mbeki as a psychopathic fool who aligned with dissident scientists to deny the link between HIV and AIDS, and they came up with statistics (Sarah Boseley, 2008;Martin Asser, 2000), to show how his arrogance contributed to the deaths of thousands of his countrymen by denying them life-saving drugs. Three years later, Mbeki presented a comprehensive plan that didn't dismiss the HIV virus, but acknowledging *poverty* as one of the key players in its transmission. His major conclusion was that focusing on HIV alone such as with condoms to prevent it and drugs to control it, was an inadequate response to AIDS in Africa. He added that addressing poverty is the ultimate way of preventing HIV Transmission. The western propaganda, often misquoting Mbeki on the link between HIV and AIDS, contributed significantly to undermining the efforts of an African to 'invent' a solution to African's problem. Unfortunately, this propaganda continued to flourish for several years (Verity Murphy, 2003, Chris McGreal 2007) and so many others, further discouraging Africans from critically analyzing their problems.

There are few opportunities left for invention or *micro*

invention I would say, particularly in rural communities that have not yet been or have been *weakly* contaminated with modern inventions. In rural areas of the coastal regions for example, people were faced by a need for a cup that has a long handle to avoid contaminating their pots when drinking fluids from it. Although untraceable, I must assume that they must have faced some problem, perhaps outbreak of diarrhoea or dysentery and there was an immediate need for this kind of a cup and someone or some people came up with such a design.

To date, the rural communities in the republic still face challenges some of which the modern inventions such as smartphones or tarmacked roads cannot address. It's unfortunate in the republic of the poor when people, particularly the politicians, think that modern technologies such as smart phones, electricity and tarmacked roads are the primary needs of the community and believe that these will solve their basic problems. While these remain important, I do not think they are the priorities. The priorities are the technologies or inventions that would allow people in the republic to maximize food production to meet their needs every year before we build roads that will be used to transport or sell the *excess* outside their communities or before you build telephone towers that will facilitate communication with customers for selling *excess* food to generate incomes. Unfortunately, the modern technologies are put in place with the assumptions that the poor will be able to transport their harvest and communicate with customers, while the technologies to maximize production of these harvests so that they sell only the excess, are weakly looked upon.

While modern inventions such as medicines and medical equipments are necessary to solve secondary needs such as need for quality health services , there is still room for invention in addressing basic or primary needs such as food, water, shelter etc. The modern inventions for farming, harvesting, storage and preparation of foods have not been accessible to these rural communities, almost after half a decade of independence in most republics; creating an opportunity for rethinking of our focus from the modern inventions to perhaps improvement of local inventions. More than ninety percent of rural societies in many republics have no access to safe and clean water , warranting a need to relook on how we can improve local inventions to address the need.Modern inventions have not been accessible for improving houses in rural communities in most republics and people are still living in semi permanent structures.Perhaps, we should promote inventions that utilize local materials to solve housing problems. People in rural communities of the republic cannot wait indefinitely for modern inventions to be accessible to them. Even if made available, not all of the poor will be able to afford them, as such; we need to focus on promoting micro inventions in these areas. The core belief is that everyone has the ability to make or do something.

Inventions have several characteristics:,One is its ability to address the need beyond the target community or population in its current shape or after being improved.. In most cases, something is invented to address a specific immediate need however; it may address beyond the target immediate need. In its current form or shape, the same invention by one of the tribe in the republic is addressing their needs for a cup with a long handle; at the same time it is also addressing my need for a traditional item to decorate my sitting room and somehow addressed the need of my western friend to learn what Africans are capable of making. When improved for example, if a rope to hang it on one's neck is added instead of a handle, the same invention may address the need of specific people that were not initially targeted such as people with no arms.

The inventions may be formal and informal. A formal invention entails the products of the formal sectors or in simple words, first and second world technologies. Informal inventions are the ones that are 'invented' in informal sectors that constitute majority in third world countries. This, the informal inventions, is what I refer to as *micro inventions*. There are a number of inventions taking place in people who are considered as poor in the republic. There are some people within these republics who keep inventing things to address the needs of their communities. This means that some people are continually using the available resources to show their potential. Unfortunately, these inventions are often not promoted and people like me and you, often see these inventions as just traditional decorations not as tools to improve other's lives in the republic of the poor. As such, they are neither mass produced for serving their intended purposes nor improved to serve new purposes.

I have worked as a public health expert in rural villages of the republic and have witnessed thousands of micro inventions in these villages. Likewise, as person who spent all my childhood in a rural village, I have participated in inventing things. When I was young, my peers were struggling with things to play with, such as the traditional toys- like those used by children in modern world. I also realized that my father, as well as theirs had neither the time nor the budget to make or buy us playing materials and I once mobilized them to gather sticks, old wires and old sandals to make 'cars' modelling a priest's car that used to visit the village for Sunday services. We invented our own handmade toys to address the need for toys that was essential for our plays ,thus stimulating our brain development. We used to drive these cars while imitating the loud sound that we have noticed coming from the priest's car.

Another need growing up was something to shoot down birds with, for two purposes; one for catching ourselves a meal and two to show off our abilities in shooting. As a result we invented v-shaped rubber-on-stick bird shooters. Those of us who were bad shooters decided to later start extracting a thick milk-like fluid from cactus trees and warmed it to make very thick glue. This glue was then covered in tree branches to trap birds that would come to rest on it. This glue, if it got into someone's eye accidentally or purposefully, the eyelids would stick together, making one unable to see for several days. Our determination however, made us take the risk. The risks that made me fail to attend a Christmas cerebrations one day after a drop of the glue stuck in my eyes for several days- yet we kept inventing to address our needs.

In one of the villages I visited in southern part of the republic where maternal mortality was high,, I found some had improved bicycles as ambulances that were essentially made of a traditional chair on the bicycle carrier tied with ropes, cushioned with animal skins- to address the problems of transporting sick people, especially pregnant mothers to the hospitals. In another village, people have   invented equipment that applied chemical distillation techniques to extract traditional brews 'chang'aa'   using hollow bamboo trees as pipes connected to big pots that contained a thick solution of fermented cereals. These people have never attended formal chemistry classes.

Back in my village, to prevent dust, cockroaches, mosquitoes and other insects from hiding in the walls of houses, we used the semi-dried cow's dung to paint the walls. This was also used to make the floor smooth. Even in places with no rocks on which cereals can be dried, the semi-dried cow's excreta was mixed with sand and painted on the ground, left to dry and used for drying cereals. For storage of cereals , a pot like structure with a grass roof and walls painted with the cow's excreta, *ekitara*, was made and put on top of pieces of rocks to prevent it from catching moistures. Pots were invented for keeping drinking water cold. To small pots for food storage,a special rope was used to hang them on a traditional ceiling.Also,a special table made of the barks of the tree, boats from the tree for fishing, a bed made of animal skin and many others are among the equipments and tools that were invented to address people's needs and they are still in use in some parts of the republic.

Unfortunately, all these cheap and simple inventions as I said earlier, are weakly promoted or not seen as important by the educated people or 'experts' in respective fields. Instead of looking for a way to improve these inventions, they would either *describe* the potential modern inventions that could serve similar purposes that are not readily available in these communities but available in modern world. They would then come up with prejudices and stereotypes for people who use these inventions or the invention itself. They would for example, see the cow excreta painted on walls as dirty or a *predisposing factor* to so many diseases and may give the 'scientific' justifications for the short term and long-term health impacts of these micro inventions. Instead of working with the people to explore the environment in order to either find contextualized alternatives or materials that can be mixed with the cow excreta to reduce the health impacts and improve its use, the experts would offer expatriate solutions that are not readily accessible within these communities.

Often, the experts would take a photo of a half-naked boy standing beside a cow dung covered house and post a big *'every dollar you give counts'* signs on their websites and life improvement proposals positively promoting the views in Binyavanga Wainaina's *How to write about Africa* . They would confidently describe the health risks of carrying a pregnant woman on bicycle ambulances, discouraging the use of these micro inventions without 'walking with the people' to explore the contextualized alternatives or modifications of these solutions since bicycles are the only available method of transport in these areas.

There was a time when the highest official of one republic promised the tricycle ambulances for rural health service units. Billions of the republic's currency units were spent in purchasing those ambulances. However, after a month or so, most of these ambulances were grounded at the health centres- entirely useless(Isangula, 2011, *Riding Birth…. Riding Death*). The modern ambulances would always require improved infrastructures and village roads (not highways) are often in bad condition in rural areas of the republic. Even in areas where the roads are in a good condition, the republic does not always have sufficient budget for running the ambulances. As such, micro inventions in rural areas seem the only hope to addressing their needs.

Women who are using the distillation techniques to make local brews are often imprisoned since it is considered 'illegal'. Neither the police nor the court provides a contextualized alternative for these women to earn income, for the consumers of these brews or a new invention that would extract the poisonous methane from local brews providing a chance for these women, like my mother, to send their sons and daughters to school.

I am not saying that people should come up with inventions that would address the needs that are considered illegal but what I am saying is that contextualized alternatives are necessary if something is to be discontinued. I will talk about this in the coming lessons.

Further Reading

1. Bamber Gascoigne. History of Inventions and Discoveries. HistoryWorld. From 2001, ongoing. http://www.historyworld.net/wrldhis/PlainTextHistories.asp?groupid=1410&HistoryID=ab23&gtrack=pthc.
2. Basil Davidson. The African Genius: An Introduction to African Culture and Social History, Boston: Little Brown and Co., 1969, p.121.

3.   Binyavanga Wainaina. How to Write About Africa. Available at http://www.granta.com/Archive/92/How-to-Write-about-Africa/Page-1

4.   Boahen, A. Adu. Africa Under Colonial Domination, 1880-1935. James Currey Publishers. 1990. p. 80

5.   Chris McGreal. Mbeki admits he is still Aids dissident six years on.2007-11-06. Available at http://www.theguardian.com/world/2007/nov/06/south africa.aids

6.   Eades, J.S. The Pre-colonial Period. The Yoruba Today. Cambridge University Press.1980.

7.   Giddens, A. (1990). The consequences of modernity. Stanford, Calif.: Stanford University Press.

8.   Godfrey Mwakikagile. Africa and the West. Nova Publishers.2000. p. 70.

9.   Isangula, K.G. Riding Birth.... Riding Death! Available at http://rural-voicestz.blogspot.com/2011/08/riding-birthriding-death.html.

10. Jenny, L. Stone Age Inventions.. Available at http://prezi.com/zqzelfwexnbv/stone-age-inventions/

11. John Iliffe. Modern History of Tanganyika. Cambridge University Press. 1979.pp. 168–172.

12. Management Sciences for Health. Business planning for Health.Building organizational Capacity to Improve Health. Participants Handbook.2013.

13. Martin Asser. South Africa Aids crisis worsens . 19th April 2000a. Available at http://news.bbc.co.uk/2/hi/health/719183.stm

14. Martin Asser. Analysis: Mbeki and the Aids sceptics. BBC News Online. 20th April 2000b.Available at http://news.bbc.co.uk/2/hi/africa/720995.stm

15. Richard Petraitis. Bullets into Water: The Sorcerers of Africa. Available http://www.reall.org/newsletter/v06/n06/bullets-into-water.html

16. Sarah Boseley. Mbeki Aids denial 'caused 300,000 deaths. The guardian. 2008-11-26. Available at http://www.theguardian.com/world/2008/nov/26/aids-south-africa

17. Verity Murphy. Mbeki stirs up Aids controversy. BBC News Online. 2003-09-26. Available at http://news.bbc.co.uk/2/hi/africa/3143850.stm

LESSON SIX

The Poor.
The Freedom of Choice.

"I don't think of myself as a poor deprived ghetto boy who made good. I think of myself as somebody who, from an early age, knew I was responsible for myself, and I had to make good"-Oprah Winfrey

In my autobiography, *Another Story...Not!* I told a story about a decision I once made when working as a clinician in one of the hospitals at the earlier stages of my career. I had to choose between operating on a pregnant woman with advanced AIDS and experiencing difficulty in giving birth, putting myself at risk of HIV or not to operate. Her prognosis was bad and the surgical facilities were unfavorable with insufficient instruments and supplies that put me at a pronounced risk of coming in direct contact with HIV infected blood. There was a chance to save the child, though in so doing , perhaps the mother or both might die. I had a choice;a choice to save myself like many of my colleagues, or choose to save at least one life at the expense of *destroying* my future. In the end I put myself at risk despite unexplainable emotional sufferings I faced during and after the surgery.

There are mixed arguments about poverty. While some argue that it is a result of failure of those who are given the task to lead others into a promised land; others argues that poverty is both congenital and hereditary that, it is something a child is born with and passed from parent to child ,while some argue that poverty is an individual choice.

Perhaps all of these arguments are true or perhaps they work synergistically. Thus, poverty may result from failure of leader who is often given authority to perform three key tasks ; providing (economic) *direction* in terms of vision and ensuring that a republic reaches there; providing *protection* by making sure the society is not vulnerable and can survive external threat whether military invasion or economical threats and; providing *order* and stability within the republic so that people spends most of their time towards achieving the (economic) vision. (Heiffetz, Grashow and Linsky, 2009)

Poverty is not a disease, it is a situation. It is a situation, which is often a result of failure to productively explore and use the resources within the reach of an individual. As far as biology is concerned, poverty is neither a congenital nor hereditary situation. According to online biology dictionary (www.biology-online.org), the word congenital means something that *is existing at and usually before birth, referring to conditions that are present at birth, regardless of their causation.*

Congenital condition refers to conditions about the biological features of an individual, and congenital problems occur to the growing foetus during early stages of development. Although these conditions can be genetic, they mostly occur due to negative impact of environmental triggers such toxins; they affect the body of a growing fetus.

Despite this definition, its seems pretty obvious that poverty contributes to increased exposure to environmental toxins as we saw in lesson two and these toxins may impair normal development, including brain development impacting intelligence in the long run.For those who want to believe that poverty is congenital, it is clear that congenital situations are situations which a baby is *born with* and not situations a baby is *born in*, the latter being poverty.

At various stages of development, the fetus may be sensitive or at risk of abnormalities and disabilities - such as congenital heart and other organ defects. Whether due to environmental factors (Koger, Schettle and Weiss 2005), the health or condition of the mother, or for unknown reasons, a growing fetus may develop an illness, disease, condition or other abnormality that will be present when he or she is born- a congenital abnormality. Most of congenital conditions cannot be passed on from the parent to child and some can be prevented. If a child is born with a congenital defect - even one that is rather severe - if he or she can procreate, the likelihood is that a normal child will result. Examples of congenital conditions may be characteristics such as less or more fingers.

On the other hand, Marian- Webster dictionary defines hereditary as a condition that is 'passed or able to be passed (genetically) from parent to child before birth' and as well the child is born with it and not born in it. A hereditary condition is one that is genetically predetermined. It entirely depends on the genetic material or chromosomes that a person inherits from one or both biological parents. A person may also be a career of an illness, disease or condition without actually having the condition. With some diseases, if a person only inherits the trait from one parent, they are said to have a recessive trait. While for some hereditary conditions, it only takes inheriting it from one parent, for others it takes inheriting the trait from both parents in order for the condition to develop. Examples of hereditary conditions are Color blindness and Sickle Cell Anemia that are passed on to a fetus from the genes of the mother and father. Since poverty cannot be passed from parents to children through gene mediated transmission, it cannot be hereditary.

The arguments at *debate.org* see poverty as a choice. One of the arguments is that if a family head gets sick, a situation that may send a family into poverty, he may decide to let the family succumb due to his sickness or choose to fight the illness and remain alive in order to support the family. And that however serious the disease may be, people would struggle not to die to avoid their family to go into poverty.

Poverty is also about attitude. Poor people who think that poverty is God-given, congenital or hereditary usually die poor. Poverty sometimes results from negative attitude about poverty itself.

An example of *negative attitude* is the way we think about death. Some people are afraid of talking about death despite the fact that the probability of dying at any given time equals to the probability of staying alive in that period. Fear of talking or even thinking about death makes life difficult for the remaining family once someone dies. People who are extremely fearful of death are fearful of the arrangements that must be made before death such as writing a will that directs the remaining members of the family how to handle the dead body and other assets. As much as we choose not to talk about death, we as well, choose to leave a lot of legal problems to the remaining members of the family. Similarly, the *negative attitudes* towards poverty, therefore makes people choose activities that facilitates them to remain in it..

Poverty is about how we deal with the challenges, or *stimulus*. Ivan Pavlov's classical conditioning experiment as described by Nevid in 2013 as well as by Belmont, Wadsworth, Watson & Rayner in 1920 shows that to every stimulus, a *challenge* or *problem* in this context, there is a natural response . Here, the key word is that there is a **natural response to a stimulus or challenges**. Although in Pavlov's ideas the natural response is considered as out of control of the responding entity, I believe that human beings as a responding entity, not dogs to whom the experiment was conducted, have the capacity to control the response depending on the nature of the stimulus. Thus, the responder can actually choose how to respond to a certain stimulus. Personally, I believe that between a stimulus and the response, there is what is called a *freedom to choose* your response as described in a wide range of motivational books. This freedom is dictated or shaped by your knowledge and skills, your imagination of the consequences-whether rewarding or non-rewarding, conscience, free will and of course ignorance.

Before you respond to a stimulus, you apply your knowledge and skills to analyze the stimulus itself and often trying to define it or figure out the reasons for the stimulus to present itself as it is. Imagine a married man sees a beautiful woman walking along the road. His knowledge of beauty helps him to compare that woman with an index figure that is, his wife or other women he has met in his life and then concludes that this one is beautiful by looking at certain physical characteristics. So here, he needs his knowledge of defining beauty to classify someone as beautiful.

The imagination of the consequences occurs when a person tries as much as possible to create images of the consequence of the response in his mind. This image may be rewarding or non-rewarding in nature. In the case of a man and a beautiful woman, a man may start imagining himself in bed with this beautiful woman and that pleasurable image may be rewarding in the sense that he feels good about it. If the image you create in your mind is rewarding, the response to a stimulus will significantly differ from if the image was not rewarding. Consider a man who is in bed with a woman that he desired for a very long time, but when it reaches a point where he need to make a decision of using or not using a condom, he creates an image in his mind of a person dying of HIV as a result of not using condom, the probability that he will choose to use one is higher provided that other factors do not operate at that time. The same man, if he creates an image of a very satisfied and relaxed man post sexual intercourse, he may choose not to use a condom.

There is also another force that operates in the cycle of freedom. This is what we call conscience or the intrinsic awareness of the right and wrong. If a married man sees a beautiful woman, despite of using his knowledge of beauty to classify her and perhaps holding a good image of having her in bed, the intrinsic knowledge of right and wrong may coerce him to realize that going for that woman is immoral and he'll respond accordingly. However, the other force which is ignorance may drive him to approach the woman even if he knows that it is wrong. This is similar to the condom use decision, as ignorance of the facts may make someone create assumptions that aim at supporting his choice even if deep inside he knows that it is wrong. It is very common for a married man to choose an immoral act even if he knows that the consequence of his choice is terrible. This is because he has the power to decide independently and freely. This also depicts the fact that, although humans have the freedom to choose the response, there are always the opposing forces to this freedom of choice and if the negative forces exceeds the forces that would have resulted to positive judgement, a person will make a choice with negative consequences.

I explained this so that you understand that poverty is a choice and the challenges we face such as poor housing, diseases, inadequate food and water and many others presents themselves to us as *stimulus* and we have the freedom to choose our course of actions. Critical thinking described in the second lesson is key to determining the appropriate course of action. Consider a person whose roof of his house is nearly falling. A falling roof is a stimulus by itself. If he holds an imagination in his mind of a person living in an iron roofed house, he will choose those activities that will lead him in the direction of building iron-roofed house. If he was an alcoholic, he may reduce alcohol intake to save for the house. On the other hand, if this man holds an image of a hopeless or helpless man who lives at God's mercy, he may start or continue choosing activities that will lead him to not changing the roof of his house.

There is a comment on the debate.org that caught my interest, posted by a member called Throwalegover. He comments, *"... people lack the mental strength, self-discipline, self-motivation, intelligence, or foresight to see a problem and fix it, or plan ahead. Therefore they remain financially less than to those whose priority it is to have good finances. Due to the fact that some lack the mentality and foresight to reach new heights, they are also of character that does not take responsibility for their own actions. Blaming everything and everyone but themselves for their own problems without regard to the fact that the problems are solely their own. And if you look closely these people would probably take credit for someone else's hard work if they thought they could get away with it"*

Henry T. Hamblin in *Within you is Power* comments *that* "the one who realizes that he possess a wonderful power that can raise him up no matter how crashed, he may never be a failure in life. No matter what happens to him, he will play the man, act a noble part, and rise from the ruins of his life".

Further Reading

1. Koger, S. M, Schettler,T and Weiss, B. Environmental Toxicants and Developmental Disabilities: A Challenge for Psychologists," American Psychologist, 2005. 60(3), pp. 243–255.

2. Nevid, J. S. . Psychology: Concepts and Applications. Belmont, CA: Wadsworth.2013.

3. Watson, J. B. & Rayner, R. (1920). Conditioned emotional reactions. Journal of Experimental Psychology, 3(1), 1–14.

4. Ronald Heiffetz, Alexander Grashow and Marty Linsky . The Theory Behind Practice: A brief introduction to the adaptive leadership Framework. An excerpt from the practice of adaptive leadership: Tools and Tactics for changing your organization and the World. Havard Business Press. 2009.

5. Is poverty a Choice? Available at http://www.debate.org/opinions/is-poverty-a-choice

The Poor.
The Consequences of their Sins.

I am going to remind you that almost all choices we make in our lives have consequences. In the previous lessons, I talked about a choice I had to make at earlier stages of my career and the consequences were obvious. Likewise, poor families in the republic face consequences of their responses to poverty challenges , depending on a path an individual chooses to take. The consequences may be specific to the response, immediately or later, isolated or combined with the consequences of other responses into an overall consequence.

Poverty itself is a consequence of so many choices people make. The choices that an individual make that may affect him or others directly or indirectly. Once the choices are made and poverty comes into play, it becomes a risk factor to many unfavorable conditions. The poverty mediated risk factors are aggregated to make everyday living a struggle; they are multifaceted and interwoven, building on and playing off one another acting synergistically (Atzaba-Poria, Pike, & Deater-Deckard 2004). Poverty, as a consequence of our choices, creates many problems that in turn create other problems making a cascade of problems.

For example, if one member in a poor family falls sick due to malaria, as a result of choosing not to sleep in an insecticide treated net, a family may be forced to sell one or some of family assets such as land to save his/her life. Selling the land may in turn lead to inadequate production of food that may results into hunger, that will in turn result into the children having poor nutrition and poor performance in school and so on. Poverty affects, not only physical and economic wellbeing but also emotional, and cognitive well-being of children and their families as (Sapolsky 2005)

Children is one of the groups of people in the republic that are highly affected by their parents' choices. Parents choices that lead to poverty affects children and result in uncertainties in terms of their immediate necessities such as food, shelter, health and academic progression. It is expected that for a child to grow into a productive adult, parents will offer the best care that will enhance brain growth and their capacity to critically analyze challenges and offer quality responses. Parents who make wrong choices would always create an environment that impairs brain development of their children consequently poor capacity in self-determination, self- drive and self-efficacy. We often encounter young adults depicting behaviors that can be traced back to their parent's behaviors.

Of course, this may be a good thing to the rulers of the republic as these children will grow up to become irresponsible adults with weak critical thinking skills and what I call poverty of the thought. They grow to become the blamers who are very fearful to take action; would depend on the government for everything; will become afraid of using personal efforts to improve their situation; and will believe that their personal development is the government's responsibility. As such, the political leaders will make sure that this feeling of *dependency* is propagated from one generation to the next. The leaders would institute efforts to drown those who mobilize or educate others to change the status quo.

Mostly, poor parents in the republics, particularly those in rural areas performed poorly in schools, as a result, they may have a negative attitude or may not be interested in their children's academic progress. One of my uncles advised me not to proceed with education when my body was struggling to adapt in a new environment resulting into frequent sickness. According to him, going on with school was wastage of time and the little resources my parents had. He died poor .

The poor have poor spending habits. They spend less on educating their children but more on things of little or no value such as alcohol. My nephew, for example, had to take his father to court because he was planning to use the cows for marrying a third wife instead of using them to cover for the school fees. After a lot of struggle and wasting time in court, my nephew managed to secure the fees but he had already lost a lot of time and as a result, he did not do well in his final examinations. Instead of looking at the factors that contributed to his failure, the community interpreted this as a curse from his father. This event fuelled fear and demotivated many school aged children from demanding school fees from their parents to avoid being cursed.

Another issue in the republic that is considered as not important is the fact that children from poor families often attend public schools with poorly maintained infrastructures such as classrooms, desks, boards, toilets and with less-qualified, less-motivated and few teachers. These conditions prevent children from learning in a safe environment. These schools often have names that reflect their appearances- named after a stone or tree, a village, a district or count, a region, and seldom a political leader. These students walk several kilometers, often barefoot and on empty stomach to school simply because of a bylaw that requires that all students attend schools. In my personal account, I walked six to eight kilometers every day to school from the age of eight. These children face a lot of uncertainties both at school and home. At school, they would sit for several hours in a classroom waiting for a teacher to show up either from the district headquarters where he was also waiting for his salary or from another classroom. At home, the uncertainties about food, cloths, shelter are imminent. Personally, the only time we enjoyed rice is during Christmas and because our stomach's enzymes were not used to such *'english'* food, we wouldn't be full by only eating rice as it was believed to be absorbed as soon as it gets in the stomach. Thus, we would always request a supplementary plate of *'Ugali'* to fill the gap. My uncle , prevented us from drinking water as soon as we ate rice since it would dissolve the precious rice making it disappear in the abdomen and that, we would feel hungry again. It became a custom for my mother to cook both rice and *Ugali* during Christmas.

On the other hand, children from well-off families are short of uncertainties. These are the children of a few percent of people in the republic who controls the country's income particularly when,according to the World Bank, a Gini Index is considered.. The names of their schools often begins with 'Saint' or 'Al-' named after holy angles, disciples of Jesus or prophet Mohammad. Their schools are well furnished, often with modern facilities and infrastructures including leisure facilities such as swimming pools. Their hands are decontaminated after several minutes , their feet are clean and their school bags are full of tasteful takeaways and so on.
A number of researches have found that there is a high risk of educational underachievement for children who are from low-income housing circumstances. This is because most parents in the republic of the poor are often unwilling to get involved in school activities or even follow up on academic progress of their children. Often, these parents or caregivers starts teaching these students entrepreneurial skills at a very young age by giving them items such as groundnuts, sweets

and cakes to sell at schools further shifting their attention from   classroom activities to business guaranteeing them lower grades. On the other hand, well off parents are very much interested in the academic progress of their children, inquiring academic reports from the teachers and would always   participate in school activities such as parents' day and so on. They willingly pay a   large school fees, and consider it an investment. Since school fees is an investment, these parents routinely monitors their children's progress as the business man would monitor his investment to make sure it is generating profit (the joy of performing well academically).

Majority of poor people in the republic never entertain luxurious events such as birthdays or parties. They have their own alternatives to such events. Their alternatives are usually traditional events such as dances that are mostly seen during the weddings. This also another opportunity for the poor to eat rice in addition to Christmas or a funeral of someone who was considered well off among them or when the dwellers of the city are brought back for burial in their home villages. The first time I cerebrated my birthday for example was the thirtieth birthday. On the other hand, the well-off families would spend millions on such things as birthdays and marriage anniversaries.

The consequence of poverty does not end at an individual and the family level, it goes beyond to the communities and the republic as a whole   (Bradley and Corwyn   2002). Children who live in poverty during the earlier stages of their development are more likely to grow into poor adults. In schools, majority will not proceed to secondary schools and universities making the education system in the republic pyramidal in terms of those who are enrolled from elementary school to universities. At the end of the day, they would turn to *unjust employment*s. Unjust employments are the type of employment that enables people to earn an income that will only suffice the basic necessities but unfairly remaining within the same level of income. The unjust employment is less likely to help an individual to move from one level of Maslow's hierarchy of need to the next and if that happens, it is more likely a result of immoral acts or choices in his career. Politicians in the republic are the motivators for the unjust employments. They would lessen the laws or bylaws to allow as many people particularly recent young graduates to enter unjust employments and at last the youth will payback during electoral campaigns.

Due to the choices the poor make, some of them for example end up having houses that is equivalent to being homeless. Some of the houses are not really houses but *sketches* of houses. Because of the choices particularly among the dwellers of the city, children become street children. The people in the slums or slum like shelters, who make up more than a third of the world's urban population, live in poverty no better or much worse, than those in rural villages (BBC News 2006). Lastly, armed robberies, child abuse, rape and many other types of violence will continue to rise as long as the poor in the republic continue to be poor.

Further Reading

1. Atzaba-Poria, Pike, & Deater-Deckard. Do risk factors for problem behaviour act in a cumulative manner? An examination of ethnic minority and majority children through an ecological perspective Journal of Child Psychology and Psychiatry.2004. 45;707–718.
2. BBC News. Report reveals global slum crisis. 2006. Available at http://news.bbc.co.uk/2/hi/5078654.stm
3. Bradley, H, R. and Corwyn, R. F. Socioeconomic Status And Child Development. Annual Review of Psychology. 2002, 53: 371-399.
4. Gini Index. World Bank. Available at http://data.worldbank.org/indicator/SI.POV.GINI
5. Robert H. Bradley and Robert F. Corwy . Socioeconomic status and child development. Annual Review of Psychology.2002. 53: 371-399.
6. Sapolsky R. Sick of poverty. Scientific America. 2005 Dec;293(6):92-9

The Poor.
Poverty as their Culture.

This is my last lesson about the republic of the poor. Partly, I feel sad because throughout this journey, I found myself creating an emotional bond with you, either as a listener or a reader of my lessons. Somehow, I believe that the end of these lessons, marks the beginning of other lessons about these republics and I am sure we will together begin a new journey soon.

Before I wind up my lessons on the poor in the republic, allow me to talk about one of the theories on the poor.

Although theories are expression of one's *ideas* that are intended to *explain* something not to *make* something happen, they are equally important since inventions for example, begins with ideas. The first thing I want to talk about is what we call the culture of poverty. The term culture of poverty was coined by Oscar Lewis in his book *The Children of Sanchez* published in 1961 and documented in his publication in 1969. He coined this term after conducting an ethnographic studies or in other words, direct observation of small Mexican communities. He uncovered a number of attributes or characteristics shared within these communities such as frequent violence, a lack of a sense of history, a neglect of planning for the future, and so on. Although one

91

of the critics of his theory is the fact that this study only covered a small number of or few communities, I consider Lewis's findings as among the available explanations of the behaviors we see in poor people in our republics. Lewis suggested that there is a universal culture of poverty and some of the characteristics of this culture is the observations that; the *people in the culture of poverty have a strong feeling of marginality, of helplessness, of dependency, of not belonging. They are like aliens in their own country, convinced that the existing institutions do not serve their interests and needs. Along with this feeling of powerlessness is a widespread feeling of inferiority, of personal unworthiness.* These were documented in his publications in 1966, 1969 and 1998. If you followed all my lessons, you will come to an understanding that concepts like helplessness, dependency and powerlessness in our republics are among the things I spend most of my time discussing . The culture of poverty constitutes,according to Lewis, what is called a *design of living* that is passed on from generation to the next. In this design of living, poor individuals feel marginalized, helpless and inferior, and adopt an attitude of living for the present or what I call living for *survival* by addressing whichever immediate need that comes along in their daily life.

Lewis,in his publications of 1966 and 1998 affirms that this culture of poverty perpetuates poverty and it often perpetuates itself from one generation to the next because of its effect on children. A child growing up in slums or slum like dwellings or those I call the dwellers of the city, by the time s/he reaches the age of six or seven,has assimilated the basic values and attitudes of parents' subculture and is not *psychologically* geared to take full advantage of changing conditions or increased opportunities which may occur in his/her lifetime. When Lewis uses the word *psychological gearing*, he is simply talking of the *thought process* and that children assimilate, largely through observation learning, the values and attitudes that represent the choices resulting from their parent's thought process. If their parent's thought process projects choices or behaviors that limit their capacity, to take full advantage of changing conditions or opportunities in their lifetime, so does the children when they grow up. In previous sections, I have explained the cascading impact of poverty on an individual, family and communities which typically explain the culture of poverty.

The theory of culture of poverty also offers another way of looking at poverty, by explaining why poverty has persisted, despite massive investments in antipoverty initiatives in many republics. While income-based supports have benefited most of non-beneficiaries, the targeted group weakly benefits. More than 70percent of the external funds often end up being used as operating costs for the so called implementing partners of the funding agencies. These implementing partners pays their staff healthier salaries almost three to ten times that of the same level civil servants plus other benefits such as expensive insurance cover, field travel costs (per diems, accommodations and fuels or flights) and so on. Also, these partners often spend more money to meet expenses for expatriate visits as well as huge office rents and utilities. At the face all these deductions, a very small percent reaches the target population where it is also slashed hierarchically before reaching the true beneficiary. It is common to find an implementing partners spending more than fifteen years in a village, district, count or regions but the changes seen are similar to what could have naturally happened even if they were not there.

I believe that the resources available in the republic are sufficient to develop the people since the colonialists used the same resources to develop their countries. However, because we are accustomed to donations from funders, I have always proposed that the world should design implementing mechanisms that removes middle entities between a funding agency and the direct beneficiary.. I have proposed that these funders can establish home support officers that will oversee implementation of the project remotely and a local implementing officer who would operate in target village or districts through thoroughly thought and designed village or district level accountability mechanisms. I believe the experts in designing implementing mechanisms cannot fail to come up with the best model of how this can work out. In my opinion, eliminating a middle entity, the implementing partner, will ensure that more that 70percent of funds that is being used to meet operating expenses could now be directed to beneficiaries. I know the world 'impossible' may be clouding your thoughts simply because eliminating the so called implementing partners and expatriates means they will become jobless. However, I feel that we can at least experiment new mechanisms since the current mechanisms have not been effective in poverty reduction or system strengthening.

While in these lessons, as well as the poverty culture theory an individual is central to persistence of poverty, critics of the theory argues that structural factors rather than individual characteristics can better explain why poverty persists. I partly agree with these critics when the structures referred to include the implementing mechanisms of donor funded program, but I strongly believe that an individual is the epicenter to persistency of poverty in our republics. You are free however, whether to agree with these criticism or stick to my belief. Even if the so called structural factors play a significant role, an individual is the key. This is evidenced by the fact that in areas where structural mechanisms are in place and that these mechanisms favors everyone equally, people will not always have the same level of income- there are those who will have more income than others supporting the idea that individual choices and efforts determines your income in any environment.

Closely related to the culture of poverty is what we call the *cycle of poverty*. This is a phenomenon where poor families become trapped in poverty for at least three generations in which the family includes no surviving ancestors who possess and can transmit the intellectual, social, and cultural capital necessary to stay out of or escape poverty (Wikipedia).

The cycle of poverty occurs when poor people lack or have insufficient resources necessary to get out of poverty, such as education that prepares students to respond to social challenges and design critically thought solutions. In other words, poverty-stricken individuals experience disadvantages as a result of their poverty, which in turn increases their poverty. As I said in previous lessons, a child born to a poor father is more likely to become a poor adult so does his children and grandchildren. Literary, this means the probability of a poor person remaining poor throughout their lives is very high. This cycle is also referred to as a pattern of behaviors and situations which cannot easily be changed by common approaches (Valentine 1968). These behaviors can only be changed by strengthening the thought process to enable individuals to critically analyze the choices they make, in order for them to get out of the cycles of poverty.

The concept of the cycle of poverty may also explain why some families who were poor become rich and their descendants may go back to poverty. An individual in a family of the poor may make certain choices and efforts in life that can at least break this cycle for a while but, if his descendant's thought process is not programmed to share his/her desires and motives, it is more likely that the following generation will go back into poverty, after exhausting the income that was generated by the efforts of their parents, making a cycle extended in terms of time but complete at the end. You might have heard of a family with a very poor grandfather but parents became rich and then children faced extreme poverty perhaps more extreme than what their parents faced before they became rich. This explanation is true if other factors such as natural disasters or wars are not linked to the change in economic status of the said parents. Generally, making choices by critically analyzing our situations, applying both divergent and convergent thinking to come up with solutions, and experimenting our solutions regardless of the risks, prepares our descendants to adopt the same values and attitudes through observation learning consequently preparing them to continually manipulate the cycles of poverty.

To this end, I believe that I have challenged your thinking and beliefs about the poor in the republic. The aim of these lessons is to challenge your thinking and opinions, so as to initiate discussions on the topic. In so doing, I have accomplished my goal.

Further Reading

1. Oscar Lewis. The Culture of Poverty. In G. Gmelch and W. Zenner, eds. Urban Life. Waveland Press.1966.
2. Oscar Lewis. Culture of Poverty. In Moynihan, Daniel P. On Understanding Poverty: Perspectives from the Social Sciences. New York: Basic Books. 1969.pp. 187–220.
3. Oscar Lewis. The culture of poverty. Society.1998. 35 (2): 7.
4. Valentine, C. A. Culture and Poverty. University of Chicago: London, 1968.
5. Wikipedia . Cycle of poverty. [online]. Available at http://en.wikipedia.org/wiki/Cycle_of_poverty

ABOUT THE AUTHOR

Kahabi G. Isangula is a medical doctor, public health expert, a researcher, a writer, a poet, a husband and a father. Born in a very small and poor village of fishermen located on the eastern shores of Lake Victoria, he has frequently been using an account of his personal experiences to motivate others. He has attended prestigious educational institutions, both in his country and western nations and spent most of his time working in both rural and urban regions of Tanzania.He authored *Another Story... Not!* , an autobiography, *Sindano inayovuja* (a Leaking Needle), *Siri za Maisha* and co-authored *'Diwani ya Kisima cha Mashairi'*, all of which are available at online bookstores.

Contacts:
Dr.Kahabi G. Isangula
P.o.Box 1252, Shinyanga,Tanzania +255
Tel: +255754030726 Fax: +255736600509
E-Mail: kaisa079@yahoo.com